CAMPAIGN 68

LÜTZEN 1632

CLIMAX OF THE THIRTY YEARS WAR

SERIES EDITOR: LEE JOHNSON

CAMPAIGN 68

LÜTZEN 1632

CLIMAX OF THE THIRTY YEARS WAR

WRITTEN BY
RICHARD BRZEZINSKI

BATTLESCENE PLATES BY
GRAHAM TURNER

OSPREY
MILITARY

First published in Great Britain in 2001 by Osprey Publishing, Elms Court, Chapel Way, Botley, Oxford OX2 9LP United Kingdom
Email: info@ospreypublishing.com

ISBN 1 85532 552 7

Editor: Lee Johnson
Design: The Black Spot

Colour bird's-eye view illustrations by The Black Spot
Cartography by The Map Studio
Battlescene artwork by Graham Turner
Originated by Grasmere Digital Imaging Ltd, Leeds, UK
Printed in China through World Print Ltd.

01 02 03 04 05   10 9 8 7 6 5 4 3 2 1

For a Catalogue of all books published by Osprey Military and Aviation please write to:
The Marketing Manager, Osprey Publishing Ltd., P.O. Box 140, Wellingborough, Northants NN8 4ZA United Kingdom
Email: info@ospreydirect.co.uk

The Marketing Manager, Osprey Direct USA,
c/o Motorbooks International, P.O. Box 1,
Osceola, WI 54020-0001, USA.
Email: info@ospreydirectusa.com

Buy online at:
www.ospreypublishing.com

KEY TO MILITARY SYMBOLS

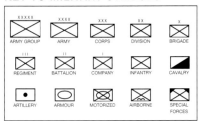

Acknowledgements

The writing of this book has been a long and arduous task involving travel to archives, libraries and museums across northern Europe and source texts in a dozen languages, often in Gothic handwriting – small wonder that the Thirty Years War is so poorly covered by historians! Just as difficult has been the tight word-limit, which has forced me to discard more material than appears in these pages.

During this protracted gestation period I have run up intellectual debts to many people. Foremost I wish to thank Keith Roberts for interesting discussions over many years; John Rohde, who helped with ideas for the battlescene artwork; Nick Sekunda for his useful comments on the manuscript; and Klaus Jacob, a modern-day resident of one of the Rippach villages, who provided information from local chronicles. In Sweden, I would especially like to thank Eva Turek of the Swedish Trophy collection, Nils Drejholt of the Livrustkammaren and Leif Pettersson of the Armémuseum for help obtaining photographs. And finally, a very large thank you to Lee Johnson, who kept faith and ensured that this book got published.

All images, unless specifically credited, are from the author's collection.

Author's Note

All dates are in the 'new style' Gregorian calendar introduced in Catholic Europe from 1582. This was 10 days ahead of the 'old style' Julian calendar employed in Sweden and Protestant Germany, so that the battle of Lützen took place on 16 November, new style, or, as still commemorated in Sweden, 6 November, old style.

Artist's Note

Readers may care to note that the original paintings from which the colour plates in this book were prepared are available for private sale. All reproduction copyright whatsoever is retained by the Publisher. All enquiries should be addressed to :

> Graham Turner, 'Five Acres', Buslins Lane, Chartridge, Chesham, Bucks, HP5 2SN United Kingdom

The publishers regret that they can enter into no correspondence on this matter.

PAGE 2 **The Schwedenstein at Lützen has marked the site of Gustav Adolf's death since very soon after the battle. It was originally just a waymarker on the Lützen–Leipzig road, recorded in a document of 1550 as the 'great stone'. There are, however, local legends that the stone was moved to the correct death site by veterans of the battle.**

PAGE 3 **Given to officers for good service, these metal effigies of the Swedish king were the predecessors of military medals awarded from the mid-17th century. Often enamelled and jewelled, they derived from the *Gnadenpfennige* (honour medallions) fashionable in Germany, intended to reinforce the personality cults of ruling princes. For many years after Gustav Adolf's death they were worn on a narrow black ribbon over one shoulder.**

CONTENTS

CHRONOLOGY

GUSTAV ADOLF IN GERMANY

27 June 1630 – Swedish fleet sails from Stockholm
6 July – Gustav Adolf lands at Peenemünde
20 May 1631 – Pappenheim storms **Magdeburg**
17 September – Battle of **Breitenfeld** – Gustav Adolf with Saxon help defeats Tilly, opening the way into central Germany
15 April – Battle of **Rain am Lech** – Gustav Adolf crosses the Lech river; Tilly is fatally wounded
16 April 1632 – Ferdinand II reinstates Wallenstein as C-in-C of Imperial forces
24 April – Gustav Adolf welcomed into Augsburg as the saviour of Protestantism
17 May – Gustav Adolf marches into Munich
25 May – Wallenstein retakes Prague
27 August – Relief force under Oxenstierna and Wilhelm of Weimar reaches Nuremberg
3/4 September – Gustav Adolf assaults Wallenstein's camp at Alte Feste
18 September – Gustav Adolf abandons the siege of Wallenstein's camp and marches south for the Danube
24 September – Gustav Adolf's and Bernhard's armies divide

PRELUDES TO THE BATTLE OF LÜTZEN

2 November – Wallenstein captures Leipzig's Pleissenburg castle
2–7 November – Gustav Adolf's and Bernhard's armies recombine at Arnstadt, south of Erfurt
6–7 November – Pappenheim's army joins Wallenstein's near Merseburg
12 November – Overawed by Wallenstein's army near Weissenfels, Gustav Adolf retires to fortify his camp at Naumburg
14 November – Wallenstein divides his army, allowing Pappenheim to leave for Halle
15 November – Gustav Adolf breaks camp before dawn (c.4am) and marches to attack Wallenstein, but is delayed by a skirmish at the **Rippach** (12–3pm).

16 NOVEMBER: BATTLE OF LÜTZEN

Midnight, 15 November – Pappenheim at Halle receives Wallenstein's order to march for Lützen
2.00am – Pappenheim sets off for Lützen with his cavalry
c.6.00am (first light) – Pappenheim's infantry and artillery depart Halle

9.00am – Rival armies come into view at Lützen
10.00am – Artillery exchanges begin as the Swedish battle line deploys
11.00am – Battle proper begins as the Swedish line makes a general advance
11.30am – Stålhandske's Finns beat off Croats from Swedish right wing. Mock formations of Imperial baggage handlers rout towards Leipzig
12.00pm – The Swedish Brigade captures the 7-gun Imperial ditch battery
12.00–12.30pm – Pappenheim arrives with his cavalry on the Imperial left wing, but is fatally wounded; the *Fahnenflucht* begins
c.1pm – Gustav Adolf is killed leading the Småland cavalry
1.00–2.00pm – The Swedish Yellow and Blue brigades are destroyed in attacks on the Imperial centre
2.00–3.00pm – Knyphausen recaptures the Imperial ditch battery and turns the guns on the Imperial left wing
c.2.30pm – Bernhard's second phase of attacks thrown back with heavy loss
3.00–3.30pm – Battle pauses while both armies reorganise for the final clash
3.30–5.00pm – Bernhard's final assault captures the windmill battery
c.6.00pm – Pappenheim's infantry under Reinach arrives
c.8.00pm (three hours after dark) – Wallenstein orders retreat on Leipzig
Midnight – Wallenstein reaches Leipzig

AFTER THE BATTLE

17 November – Bernhard marches back to Weissenfels and the Naumburg camp
18 November – Wallenstein abandons Leipzig and begins his withdrawal to Bohemia
22 November – 5,000 Saxon and Brunswick-Lüneburg horse join Bernhard at Grimma: mopping-up operations in Saxony begin
16 February 1633 – Execution of the Lützen routers in Prague
23 April – **Heilbronn League** formed with Axel Oxenstierna as Director-General
8 July – Protestant victory at Battle of **Hessisch-Oldendorf**
25 February 1634 – Wallenstein **assassinated**; Gallas takes over his command
6 September – Battle of **Nördlingen**: catastrophic defeat of the Protestant-Swedish army: the Swedes lose southern and central Germany
30 May 1635 – **Peace of Prague** brings to an end the 'Swedish phase' of the war. Elector Johann Georg of Saxony abandons the Swedish alliance in return for the province of Lusatia.

INTRODUCTION

The battle of Lützen was a key turning point of the Thirty Years War (1618–48), Europe's most destructive conflict before World War I. The battle was not especially large: Breitenfeld in 1631 had nearly double the number of combatants; nor was it particularly decisive – for some time both sides claimed victory. Its importance lay rather in the death of two of history's great captains: King Gustav II Adolf of Sweden and Count Gottfried Heinrich von Pappenheim.

Much remains shrouded in the mist and smoke of that cold November day. Historians have concentrated their research on the Swedish King's death; less effort has been made to unravel the progress of the battle itself. The military systems of the day remain poorly understood, and the battle is still often presented as the confrontation

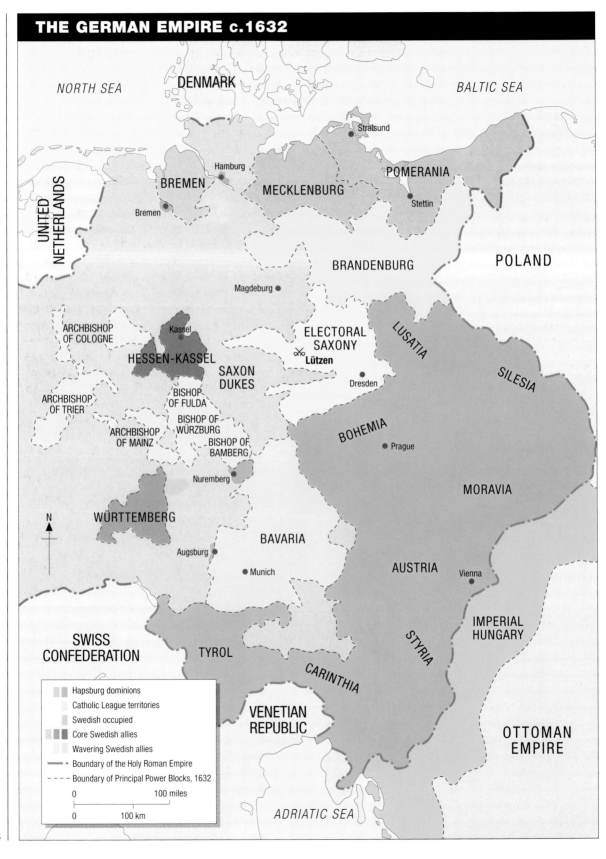

THE GERMAN EMPIRE c.1632

NORTH SEA

BALTIC SEA

DENMARK

Stralsund

Hamburg

BREMEN

POMERANIA

MECKLENBURG

Stettin

Bremen

UNITED NETHERLANDS

BRANDENBURG

POLAND

Magdeburg

ARCHBISHOP OF COLOGNE

Kassel

ELECTORAL SAXONY

LUSATIA

HESSEN-KASSEL

Lützen

SILESIA

SAXON DUKES

Dresden

ARCHBISHOP OF TRIER

BISHOP OF FULDA

BOHEMIA

ARCHBISHOP OF MAINZ

BISHOP OF WÜRZBURG

Prague

BISHOP OF BAMBERG

Nuremberg

MORAVIA

WÜRTTEMBERG

N

BAVARIA

Augsburg

AUSTRIA

Vienna

Munich

IMPERIAL HUNGARY

SWISS CONFEDERATION

TYROL

STYRIA

CARINTHIA

VENETIAN REPUBLIC

OTTOMAN EMPIRE

Hapsburg dominions
Catholic League territories
Swedish occupied
Core Swedish allies
Wavering Swedish allies
Boundary of the Holy Roman Empire
Boundary of Principal Power Blocks, 1632

0   100 miles

0   100 km

ADRIATIC SEA

LEFT **Seventeenth-century Germany was splintered into over 1,000 semi-independent political units, some of them little more than the private estates of knights or counts. In theory, the 'Holy Roman' emperor had power over this chaotic collection of states. He was chosen by the vote of seven Electors: the archbishops of Cologne, Trier and Mainz; the Dukes of Brandenburg and Saxony, the King of Bohemia, and the Pfalzgraf (or Count Palatine). It was the Pfalzgraf's acceptance of the crown of Bohemia, and with it a second electoral vote, that finally pushed the Empire into all-out war. With the conquest of the Pfalzgraf's lands after the battle of White Mountain (1620), the Pfalz vote was transferred to the Duke of Bavaria in 1623. Catholic forces in Germany were answerable either to the Catholic League (the 'Leaguists'), whose main members were the three Archbishop-electors and Bavaria, or to the Habsburg emperor (the 'Imperialists').**

between Gustav Adolf's innovative linear tactics, reliant on firepower and shock, and the obsolete Spanish school with its lumbering *tercio* formations and caracoling cavalry. Such dogma is only slowly eroding away. Another difficulty has been the bias of earlier generations of north European (that is, Protestant) historians, who habitually exaggerated the talents of Gustav Adolf and underplayed those of Wallenstein.

This book is more than a rehash of earlier histories. So much myth has embellished the tale that it was impossible to trust 19th- and 20th- century interpretations of the battle. I have gone back to the primary sources, to accounts written, as far as possible, by participants, including several that were previously unknown. I have also examined most of the prints and paintings depicting the battle.

I revert to the traditional view that Gustav Adolf died on the Swedish right wing, not the left, and refute the idea that his death spurred his troops to revenge; indeed his demise was successfully covered up. Traditional accounts see the battle as one continuous haze, though there was a half-hour lull, and even moments when the rival armies were running away from each other. New heroes emerge in the guise of generals Knyphausen and Holk, whose tireless energies kept both armies from the brink of collapse.

The key to my account has been a meticulous analysis of the armies – the regiments, their colonels and where they deployed in the battle line. The bare bones of these labours are given in the Orbat tables and diagrams. To save space, footnotes are supplied only where my interpretation is at odds with current opinion.

THE ROAD TO LÜTZEN

When Gustav Adolf landed in Germany in July 1630 the odds were stacked against him. He could supply his army only with great difficulty and had few allies. Most Germans dismissed him as another upstart northerner, who would quickly be vanquished by Tilly's invincible army. The first months proved difficult indeed and it was not until spring 1631 that the Swedish beachhead in Pomerania and Mecklenburg was secure and the King's advance south could begin.

With the storming of Magdeburg by Imperial forces in May 1631 in which 20,000 civilians died, public opinion began to turn against the Habsburg Emperor. Bremen, Brandenburg and the biggest prize of all, Saxony, signed alliances with the Swedes soon after. The scale of Gustav Adolf's victory over Tilly at Breitenfeld on 17 September 1631 came as a surprise to all. Tilly made the mistake of underestimating his enemy and paid for it with the bulk of his veteran army. The once reluctant Protestant dukes and princes of Germany now beat paths to the Swedish King's door and offered to raise troops for his cause.

With his position strengthened Gustav Adolf next struck south-west into the German heartlands, down the so-called 'Cleric's Alley' (Pfaffengasse), through the Catholic bishoprics of Fulda, Bamberg and Würzburg, and on to the wealthy city of Frankfurt am Main, crowning

'Wallenstein's Laughter'. After endless complaints from the princes of Germany, Wallenstein was dismissed from office in September 1630 and replaced as commander of Imperial forces by Tilly. During 1631 Wallenstein did his utmost to undermine Tilly's position, even denying provisions for his troops, and it was rumoured that he laughed when Tilly was killed, knowing he could now dictate terms to the Emperor. From a 1632 broadsheet entitled Wallenstein's Laughter. (Uppsala University Library)

The Imperial Free City of Nuremberg was one of Germany's wealthiest towns, a merchant hub and centre of the arms trade. The city had opened its gates to Gustav Adolf in March 1632 and provided him with financial subsidies and troops. Operating from nearby Bohemia, Wallenstein knew if he moved on Nuremberg, the Swedish King would have no choice but to come to its defence. (Early 20th-century commercial photograph by Ernst Roepke of Wiesbaden)

the successful 1631 campaign with the capture of Mainz, seat of one of the three Archbishop-Electors.

Southern Germany, in particular the crippling of Catholic Bavaria, was the King's goal for the early part of 1632. On 15 April 1632, near the Swabian town of Rain, Gustav Adolf stormed across the river Lech, fatally wounding Tilly, and then marched triumphant into Augsburg, the home of the Lutheran creed, where he was received as the 'Lion of the North' – the saviour of Protestantism. Accompanying him was Pfalzgraf Friedrich V, the dispossessed 'Winter King' of Bohemia, whose acceptance of the Bohemian crown in 1619 had escalated the conflict into a 'German War'; the recovery of the Pfalzgraf's lands now seemed assured. On 17 May Gustav Adolf marched into Munich. There seemed to be little to prevent him from walking straight into the Imperial capital, Vienna, and deposing the Habsburg Emperor Ferdinand II, but that was not to be.

Wallenstein's reinstatement & the Nuremberg campaign

In desperation Ferdinand II had already turned to the great mercenary recruiter Albrecht von Wallenstein, Duke of Friedland. Despite his extravagant demands there was no option but to ask him back. With his Bohemian estates at risk from Saxon armies, Wallenstein had already set in motion his prodigious resources, rebuilding shattered Imperial regiments and stockpiling military supplies. Within weeks of his reinstatement as 'Generalissimo' of the Emperor's forces, Wallenstein was ready to march, and by the end of May 1632 he had recaptured Prague from the Saxons. By the late spring he had recovered the rest of Bohemia, was pressuring Saxony, and was ready to strike at the Swedish King.

11

NORTH SEA

BALTIC SEA

1. 6 July 1630: Gustav Adolf lands at Peenemünde

Kolberg

Stralsund

Peenemünde

Rostock

Wolgast

POMERANIA

Stettin

Damm

Hamburg

2. 19 March 1631: Tilly storms Neu-Brandenburg

Neu-Brandenburg

MECKLENBURG

Bärwald

Oder

Bremen

6. 6 August 1631: Tilly attempts to storm Gustav Adolf's fortified camp at Werben

Werben

BRANDENBURG

Elbe

5. 27 July 1631: Four imperial horse regiments destroyed in a night action by Gustav Adolf's cavalry near Burgstall

Burgstall

Havel

Berlin

Frankfurt an der Oder

4. 20 May 1631: Tilly storms Magdeburg

Magdeburg

Weser

3. 13 April 1631: Frankfurt an der Oder stormed by Gustav Adolf's troops

Saale

7. 17 September 1631: Battle of Breitenfeld: Combined Swedish-Saxon army defeats Tilly's veterans

Spree

Kassel

Fulda

Breitenfeld

Leipzig

SAXONY

Dresden

Lützen

11. 16 November 1632: Gustav Adolf meets Wallenstein at Lützen

Erfurt

Naumburg

Weimar

Elbe

Arnstadt

Mulde

Elster

Thüringer-Wald

Königshofen

Hof

Eger

Frankfurt am Main

"Cleric Alley"

Coburg

Prague

Mainz

Schweinfurt

Eger

Moldau

BOHEMIA

Würzburg

Rhine

Main

Regnit

8. 18 October 1631: Swedes take Würzburg by storm

Windsheim

Alte. Feste

Nuremberg

FRANCONIA

Fränk Jura

10. 3 September 1632: Alte Feste: Gustav Adolf's assault on Wallenstein's fortified camp near Fürth is repulsed with heavy losses

9. 15 April 1632: Battle of Rain: Gustav Adolf forces a crossing of the Lech; Tilly is fatally wounded

Rain

Ingolstadt

Donauwörth

BAVARIA

Danube

Neckar

Danube

SWABIA

Augsburg

Lech

Munich

N

Major storming operations (Imperial)

Major storming operations (Swedish)

Important Battles

March Route 1630

March Route 1631

March Route 1632

| 0 | 50 miles |
| 0 | 100 km |

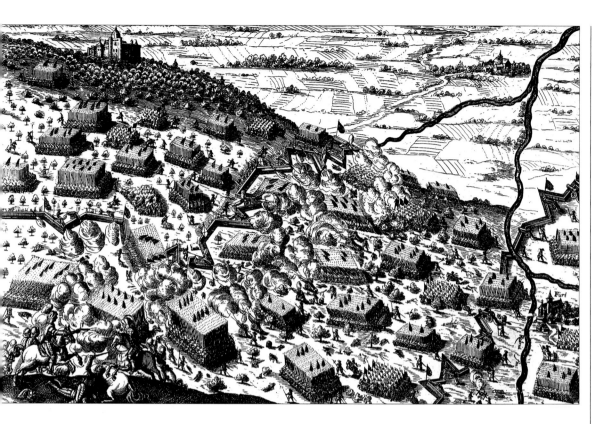

Gustav Adolf's decision to fight out the contest with Wallenstein near Nuremberg was arguably his largest blunder of the German campaign. Outnumbered by Wallenstein, he quickly found himself the besieger besieged. The Swedish chancellor Axel Oxenstierna scraped together a relief force, which arrived before Nuremberg at the end of August. The Protestant army bloated to more than 45,000 – the largest force Gustav Adolf ever fielded – and was now sufficient to challenge Wallenstein, but the condottiere had no intention of fighting an open battle, and remained resolutely entrenched in his camp.

With inadequate provisions for his vast army, Gustav Adolf had to quickly force a conclusion. When reports came on 3 September that Wallenstein appeared to be abandoning his camp, Gustav Adolf improvised an attack on the camp's steep northern ramparts near the derelict fortress of Alte Feste. The assault was a dismal failure, costing 1,000 dead and 1,500 wounded, including several key officers. The setback was trivial compared with the disaster that unfolded over the following fortnight. Camp conditions, already squalid after a long hot summer, became intolerable. Disease ravaged the troops; horses starved by the thousand; whole companies deserted along with their officers. With his army disintegrating the King clung too long to the hope that he could draw Wallenstein out to fight.

Finally Gustav Adolf accepted his mistake. After solemnly celebrating the anniversary of Breitenfeld on 17 September, the Swedish army broke camp on the 18th and withdrew southwards, to complete the conquest of Swabia and Bavaria. Wallenstein waited a few days, then set off north-east towards Bamberg and Saxony. The two rival armies would not meet again for nearly two months.

The battle at Alte Feste (3–4 September 1632). This cluttered print, made in 1633, attempts to convey the drama of the event rather than accurate details. The Swedish infantry assault columns were unable to reach the ramparts because of the intensity of fire, and were then struck by a cavalry sally, which caused such butchery that the Imperial horsemen had trouble returning over the Swedish bodies.

13

THE OPPOSING COMMANDERS

THE PROTESTANT COMMANDERS

King Gustav II Adolf of Sweden (1594–1632) was one of the greatest men of his age and arguably modern Europe's greatest general until Napoleon toppled him from that pedestal. Both in legend and reality, he was larger than life: blond and tall, his presence and charisma impressed everyone who met him. He spoke half a dozen languages, was cultured and erudite, and yet had the modesty to banter with his ordinary soldiers.

He was born in 1594, to a German mother, daughter of Duke Adolf of Holstein-Gottorp, and a Swedish father, Karl, Duke of Södermanland (from 1607 Karl IX of Sweden), third son of King Gustav I Vasa; his

Gustav II Adolf Vasa, King of Sweden (1594–1632). The 'Lion of the North' is depicted here at the height of his career after the entry to Frankfurt am Main in November 1631. Though becoming stout on the rich German diet, he was still (aged a few weeks short of 37), a relatively young man. (Posthumous portrait attributed to Mattaeus Merian junior, Skokloster, Sweden)

ABOVE, LEFT **Duke Wilhelm of Sachsen-Weimar (1598–1662). An experienced soldier who had fought in earlier phases of the war, Gustav Adolf appointed him General-leutnant and second-in-command of Swedish forces in Germany, soon after Breitenfeld. But his heart was not in the task. Claiming ill-health he left the army after the Nuremberg débâcle, and handed over command to his more bellicose younger brother, Bernhard. (From** *Theatrum Europaeum***)**

ABOVE, RIGHT **Duke Bernhard of Sachsen-Weimar (1604–39), like many soldiers of his time, rose to high rank at a young age. By the time he took his first independent field command in the summer of 1632, he had already seen ten years of service. He was perhaps not a first-rate commander, but was certainly one of the most courageous that Germany produced during the war. (Portrait dated 1638 by J.E. Schäfler, Karlbergs Slott, Stockholm)**

double-barrelled Christian name, often Latinised to Gustavus Adolphus, was given in honour of his grandfathers.

From his earliest years Gustav Adolf was surrounded by strife, his family and country ripped apart by conflict. In his adulthood hardly a year passed in which he was not involved in war or planning one; first Denmark, Russia, then Poland. His upbringing had prepared him well for a military life, to the extent that he relished war and dreamed of conquest.

Sweden at the turn of the 17th century was poor and backward, but had vast untapped, natural mineral resources. Gustav Adolf's transformation of the country into a Baltic empire relied heavily on the development of the mining and metallurgy industries, but this proceeded slowly. Over the years he gave Sweden's military system a thorough shake-out, but he did so with Lutheran frugality. As much as possible was homegrown: his soldiers were conscripted from the local peasantry and uniformed in homespun cloth; armour and weapons were provided from his newly created factories. He himself dressed simply 'without any pompous or vaine-glorious shew'.

Though his reforms were conducted with frugality, they were marked by his characteristic attention to detail – as one of his Scottish officers, Robert Monro, noted, 'He thought nothing well done which he had not done himself.' In his efforts to turn Sweden into a modern state Gustav Adolf left no stone unturned, reforming all aspects of life, from law and education to civil finance and administration. Even Chancellor Axel Oxenstierna, who had a large hand in the reform programme, was shocked by Gustav Adolf's tireless energy: 'If we were all as hot as your Majesty, we should burn.'

A deep piety imbued everything that Gustav Adolf did and his soldiers revered him with an almost messianic awe. Like Cromwell after him, he used religion as an instrument of military discipline. Thanks to his Articles of War, which forbade swearing, drunkenness and whoring, he was able (at least for a time) to curb the endemic pillaging and barbaric cruelty to civilians that so plagued other armies of the period.

The original aims of Gustav Adolf's intervention in Germany were far more than a crusade for justice for the Protestants. As he said in his farewell address in Stockholm, he had been 'goaded into it by the Imperial faction' (in particular, an Imperial fleet on the Baltic, operating out of Western Pomerania) and his goal was to secure Sweden from the threat of foreign aggression. This aim could not be achieved without establishing a permanent foothold in north Germany; but his ambitions did not stop with Western Pomerania. When Gustav Adolf began handing out conquered Catholic lands as rewards to his generals, the Protestant princes knew he had come to stay and not all of them liked the fact.

In his history of the 'German War' the official Swedish historian, Chemnitz, summed up Gustav Adolf's generalship in the following terms: 'He was careful in his deliberations, prompt in his decisions, undaunted in heart and spirit, strong of arm and ready to command and fight ... Nobody could better appraise the enemy, judge accurately the chances of war, and quickly reach an advantageous solution on the spur of the moment.' The truth was that the King's risky personal reconnaissances had got him into trouble more than once. He still carried a musket ball in his neck courtesy of a Polish sniper at Dirschau (1627), and a cannon ball killed his horse when he rode too close to the Bavarian fortress of Ingolstadt during a failed siege attempt in April 1632. At Lützen his desire to direct the proceedings from the front line was to get him in more serious trouble.

Bernhard, Duke of Sachsen-Weimar (1604–16) the eleventh son of Duke Johann of Sachsen-Weimar, was born into one of Germany's foremost martial families. He distinguished himself in battle at Wimpfen (1622), before studying siegecraft in the Netherlands in 1623, and entering Danish service in 1626. His plan to create a Protestant German army led by Germans began to take shape under Hessian colours in 1631. After an heroic incident during Tilly's attack at Werben in August 1631, Gustav appointed him colonel of his German cavalry lifeguard.

The Swedes quickly appreciated Bernhard's talents, and after a brief spell as military adviser to Chancellor Oxenstierna, he was appointed generalmajor of the army in Swabia, and in September 1632 took over his brother Duke Wilhelm's field army, his first independent command. His courage and enthusiasm quickly won him the hearts of Gustav Adolf's troops, in particular the German element, who, unhappy with the Swedish King's increasingly apparent loftiness, turned to him as their natural leader.

Dodo von Innhausen und zu Knyphausen (1583–1636) has long been maligned by historians as an old and overcautious man who at Lützen advised breaking off the action at the first hint of trouble. In reality he was Gustav Adolf's most experienced and valued military professional. After an apprenticeship in Dutch service (where he held a captaincy from 1603), he served under 'Mad' Christian of Brunswick and Count Ernst von Mansfeld, witnessed the Protestant defeats at Höchst (1622) and Stadtlohn (1623) and was captured by Wallenstein at Dessau Bridge (1626). In 1628 he served England during the La Rochelle expedition, before going on to raise troops for Sweden in 1630. Gustav Adolf trusted him with all the 'impossible' jobs: making him governor of Neubrandenburg (where he was captured in 1631), and of Nuremberg in 1632. From his position in command of the reserve at Lützen, Knyphausen cast something of a fatherly influence over Gustav Adolf and the fiery young Duke Bernhard.

THE CATHOLIC COMMANDERS

Few generals were as different from Gustav Adolf, as was **Albrecht Eusebius Wenzel von Waldstejn**, a name softened in his own day to 'Wallenstein'. He was as introverted and obsessive as Gustav Adolf was outgoing and straightforward. According to astrology in which he put great stock, he was ruled by Saturn – closed, retentive; quite the opposite of the Jovian Gustav Adolf.

Dodo von Innhausen und zu Knyphausen (1583–1636). Having lived through many of the Protestant defeats in the early phases of the German War, Knyphausen was acutely aware of the risks of fighting a pitched battle. Even so he was a competent field commander and could be unhesitatingly daring when it mattered. At Lützen he was 'Generalmajor of the King's Army' and third in line of command, and took charge of the army for two critical hours at the height of the battle. (From *Theatrum Europaeum*, Vol. III)

RIGHT **Feldmarschal Gottfried Heinrich Graf (Count) zu Pappenheim (1594–1632).** One of the most intriguing and charismatic personalities of the Thirty Years War, he was courageous, dashing and self-willed to the verge of insubordination, but was also a literate man of great charm and wit. The Swedish King used to say that Tilly was an old corporal, Wallenstein a madman, but Pappenheim was a soldier, and that he feared no enemy soldier except that 'scarface'. (From *Theatrum Europaeum*)

Albrecht Eusebius von Wallenstein (Waldstein, Waldstejn), Duke of Friedland and Mecklenburg (1583–1634). Despite the familiar heroic portraits by Van Dyck (who never saw him in the flesh), Wallenstein was, in real life, physically unimpressive – sallow featured and of middling height, his wiry build contorted by gout. But behind the brooding gaze was an agile mind of unfathomable complexity and undeniable genius. (Anonymous painting formerly in Stadtrat, Nuremberg, believed lost in WWII)

Born in Hermanitz, Bohemia, Wallenstein was a Czech Protestant from a minor noble family, and was orphaned young. He changed his faith to ensure advancement in Habsburg service and married a rich wife in 1609, who conveniently died five years later leaving him extensive estates in Bohemia. He remained loyal to Ferdinand II during the Bohemian revolt, and was a colonel at White Mountain in 1620; as a reward, the Emperor let him buy up the estates of exiled Protestants at knock-down prices and made him Duke of Friedland.

At the outbreak of the Danish War in 1625, Wallenstein, now one of the richest men in Europe, contracted to raise an army at his own cost for the impecunious Emperor. His profit would come from the war itself and 'contributions' extracted from German towns – as his opponents objected, it was daylight robbery made legal by the Emperor's seal.

Wallenstein transformed his private domains in north-east Bohemia into a vast military depot, building workshops and factories to supply arms and clothing for his troops. His attention to the minutiae of logistics bordered on the obsessive; as Watts commented, 'The Duke of Friedland's Master-piece, is to be a good provisioner: and he hath a singular good Catering-wit …' More than any general before him Wallenstein realized that war was best conducted as an economic enterprise, and he did so on an industrial scale never seen before. It was him, rather than Gustav Adolf, who effected an increase in the size of European armies.

In 1629 Wallenstein received the Duchy of Mecklenburg as a reward for his services in the Danish War, but the German princes began to object to the power concentrated in his hands, his exploitative methods and even the excessive ostentation with which he surrounded himself. In September 1630 the Emperor caved in and dismissed him from office.

By the generous terms of his reinstatement to supreme command in 1632 Wallenstein achieved most of his ambitions. He had wealth, vast estates and power to rival the Emperor. But he was 11 years senior to the Swedish King, gout-ridden and already tired.

Wallenstein was respected and feared by his soldiers, rather than loved. He was generous to those who won his favour, dishing out gold ducats and promotions like confetti, but terrible and unforgiving when crossed. Whereas Gustav Adolf spurred his men to valour with charisma and religious ardour, Wallenstein ruled with the carrot and stick.

Wallenstein's saturnine character spilled over into his generalship. He disliked taking chances in the open field and preferred fighting from the security of field works. At his first major battle, Dessau Bridge in 1626, his carefully constructed earthworks proved the undoing of the other great Thirty Years War condottiere, Ernst von Mansfeld. At Alte Feste, Wallenstein ordered his men to 'make more use of their trenches than of their weapons' – to the discomfiture of an even better general. At Lützen, Wallenstein was caught off balance but, characteristically, still attempted to fight a defensive battle from an entrenched position.

Feldmarschal Gottfried Heinrich Graf (Count) zu Pappenheim (1594–1632) was, in contrast to Wallenstein, an archetypal cavalryman. A Bavarian-born convert to Catholicism, he served the Catholic League in the Bohemian War of 1620 before raising a horse regiment for Duke Maximilian of Bavaria in 1622. His brutal suppression of the 1626 Upper Austrian Peasant Revolt and successes in the Danish War got him noticed, but he was considered too headstrong and

impetuous to have a major field command, and spent much of his career playing side-kick to Count Tilly. Although adored by his troops, Pappenheim was not all sweetness. If anyone should carry the blame for the massacre at Magdeburg, it was him. Indeed he was also largely the cause of Tilly's ill-advised attack at Breitenfeld, compounding the error with charge after futile charge against the tight-knit Swedish lines. His personal bravery was never in question and he is said to have killed 14 of the enemy with his own hand in the battle.

In 1632 Pappenheim made up for his mistakes in the kind of warfare to which his unique talents were ideally suited. With a ramshackle force of a few thousand troops, he turned the Lower Saxony region of north-west Germany into his private stomping-ground, pinning down Protestant forces many times the size of his own. Using internal lines to their maximum advantage, his constant raiding (and the incompetence of Swedish commanders sent to stop him) distracted Gustav Adolf from his conquests in southern Germany. Recalled by Wallenstein to Saxony against his will, Pappenheim's bravado got him killed before he was able to make any impact on the course of the battle of Lützen.

With Wallenstein's gout causing him trouble, he was relying increasingly on **Heinrich Holk (1599–1633)** for the everyday administration of his army. A Danish Protestant, Holk had risen rapidly in Wallenstein's service, being promoted on 24 August 1632 to Feldmarschal-leutnant, a new rank (slightly junior to Pappenheim) created, it was said, specially for him.

Holk was *the* expert of war by devastation. In a conflict famous for its atrocities his troops earned an appalling reputation for brutality as they raped and pillaged their way through Saxony in late 1632. Nevertheless, flint-hearted Holk was a firm disciplinarian and an able tactician and administrator, able to satisfy even Wallenstein's elevated demands. During the battle he was everywhere at once, ordering, cajoling, shouting. Without Holk, Lützen may well have had a far more disastrous outcome for the Imperialists.

Heinrich Holk (1599–1633) was a Danish professional soldier who lost an eye in battle against the Imperialists in 1626. After the Peace of Lübeck (1629), which took Denmark out of the war, he found service with his former enemy. After catching Wallenstein's attention in 1632, he advanced rapidly from Oberst (Colonel) to Feldmarschall in just nine months. At Lützen he commanded the left wing of the army during Pappenheim's absence. (Portrait by Karell van Mander, from a private Danish collection)

OPPOSING ARMIES

OFFICER RANKS

Imperial/Saxon	Swedish	English
Generalissimus/Oberst-Kapitän	General af Armén	Captain-general
General-leutnant (GenLt)	Generalleutnant	Lieutenant general
Feldmarschall (FM)	Fältmarskalk	Field Marshal
Feldmarschall-leutnant (FMLt)		
General über der Kavallerie / über die Infanterie	General för Kavalleriet/ Fotfolket	General of the Horse/ Foot
General-feldzeugmeister (GenFZM)	General för Artilleriet	General of the Ordnance
Generalwachtmeister (GenWm)	Generalmajor	(Sergeant-) Major-general
Oberst	Överste	Colonel
Oberstleutnant (Obstlt)	Överstelöjtnant	Lieutenant colonel
Oberstwachtmeister (ObstWm)	Major	(Sergeant-)Major
Rittmeister	Ryttmästare	Captain (Horse)
Hauptmann/Kapitän	Kapten	Captain (Foot)

While campaigning in Germany the Swedes adopted German as their language of administration, so only native Swedes have been titled in Swedish.

THE SWEDISH ARMY

I n 1630 when Gustav Adolf set foot in Germany he was leading a genuinely 'Swedish' Army: It contained more German and Scots mercenaries than ethnic Swedes, but was administered by the Swedish Crown. The character and size of the army changed rapidly after Breitenfeld, which brought tens of thousands of Germans into the ranks. By November 1632 the King commanded 150,000 troops in Germany alone.

Raised by conscription and rigorously trained, the Swedish regiments were some of Gustav Adolf's best troops, and were among the first in Europe to have regional identities. Most of the Swedish and Finnish infantry had been left guarding lines of communications with Stockholm, so that at Lützen, of the 18,000 troops present, they numbered just one-quarter of the cavalry and one-tenth of the infantry.

The elite of the German units were the four 'Colour Regiments' – Yellow, Blue, Red and Green – formed between 1624 and 1627, and named after the colour of their flags (and, later, uniform jackets). Several regiments raised after 1629 also adopted colour names; the majority, however, continued to be named after their colonel (*Oberst*). After Breitenfeld many Protestant German princes offered to raise regiments at their own expense. These troops later formed the core of Duke Bernhard of Weimar's army, and became known as the 'Weimarians'.

Gustav Adolf's allies loaned him several regiments during the summer crisis of 1632. Hessen-Kassel contributed two regiments of foot and four of horse. Electoral Saxony sent two of horse (Prince Ernst of

The Swedish infantry brigade was Gustav Adolf's answer to the Spanish *tercio*. Conceived as a moving fortress with all-round defence, it was patterned on the military architecture of the day. A general shortage of pikemen had reduced it from four squadrons to three by the time of Breitenfeld, where it performed well. The Lützen fog provided a much harsher test: this time not everything went so smoothly. (Detail of the 1634 Siege of Landshut from *Theatrum Europaeum*).

Anhalt's and Hofkirchen's) and three of foot (Pforte's, Dam von Vitzthum's and Bose's). The Saxons had deployed separately from the Swedes at Breitenfeld, but were integrated into the battle order at Lützen, the infantry even adopting the Swedish brigade formation.

Last but not least were the British troops, which Gustav Adolf held in special esteem. By November 1632, his British infantry even outnumbered the ethnically Swedish infantry in Germany. Only one British regiment was at Lützen, Ludovick Leslie's, which contained the remnants of three Scottish and three English units. Many of the Marquis of Hamilton's discharged officers had also remained with the army awaiting vacant positions, and acted as ADCs during the battle.

Gustav Adolf's best cavalry were his Swedish nationals. They were now better mounted than at Breitenfeld (where Tilly had made fun of their small Scandinavian horses), and had suffered little at Nuremberg thanks to preferential foddering (much to the disgust of the German horse). Most feared of all were Stålhandske's light-armed Finns, the 'Hackapells' (named after their war-cry *Hakkaa päälle* – Hack 'em down!), who took no prisoners.

Gaelic soldiers of Alexander Hamilton's Irish/Scottish regiment, part of James, Marquis of Hamilton's ill-fated German Expedition, which disembarked at Stettin in August 1631. Survivors from this regiment fought at Lützen as part of Ludovick Leslie's regiment. (Print by Georg Köler of Nuremberg)

The German cavalry were a very mixed bunch, ranging from regiments like Courville's and Öhm's which had fought in the Polish campaign, to hastily recruited units that had yet to be issued standards. On the whole they were distinctly inferior to the Imperial horse, and it was for this reason that Gustav Adolf always strengthened them by 'interlining' bodies of musketeers between the squadrons.

The key to the success of the Swedish infantry was training. Discipline made possible the so-called 'Swedish salvo'– the simultaneous discharge of a unit's muskets at point-blank range (as little as 5–10 paces) before charging in with the sword and musket butt. Traditionally the pike was the battle-winning arm, but the reality was different. Few men were willing to serve as pikemen, many cast away their cumbersome 5 metre-long pikes on the long marches. The formal ratios of pike to shot became meaningless once an army had spent a few months in the field.

Gustav Adolf took special interest in the development of his artillery, and thanks to Sweden's abundant metal reserves, had transformed it into his battle-winning arm. With specialists recruited across Europe he developed new alloys to make lighter barrels, and standardised on just three calibres of field pieces: 24-pdrs, 12-pdrs and the famous 3-pdr regimental cannon.

For further details on the Swedish Army see the author's two volumes in Osprey's Men-at-Arms series, *The Army of Gustavus Adolphus*, (London, 1991–93) (MAA 235 and 262).

SWEDISH ORDER OF BATTLE

Commander-in-chief
Gustav II Adolf, King of Sweden

Second-in-command
'General-leutnant of the army' (acting) [1] Bernhard, Duke of Sachsen-Weimar

Third-in-command
'Generalmajor of the army' Dodo v. Innhausen und zu Knyphausen

RIGHT WING
King Gustav II Adolf

Front line
Överste Torsten Stålhandske

Småland Horse – Överste Fredrik Stenbock
8 coys, 400 horse
Östgöta Horse – Överstelöjtnant Lennart Nilsson Bååt
4 coys, 100 horse
Uppland Horse – Överstelöjtnant Isaak Axelsson 'Silfversparre'
4 coys, 250 horse
Södermanland Horse – Överste Otto Sack
4 coys, 200 horse
Västgöta Horse – Överste Knut Soop
8 coys, 400 horse
Finland Horse – Överste Torsten Stålhandske
8 coys, 500 horse (deployed in two squadrons)

Commanded musketeers – Oberst Caspar Graf v. Eberstein [2]
5 bodies each with c.200 musketeers and two 3-pdr regimental guns

Rear line
Oberst [3] Claus Conrad Zorn v. Bulach

Georg v. Uslar's Horse Regt – Oberst Georg v. Uslar [4]
8 coys, 160 horse
Hessian Horse (Composite Squadron)
Oberst Franz Elgar v. Dalwigk
Rostein's (Hessians), Oberst Friedrich Rostein, 5 coys, 180 horse
Kurt v. Dalwigk (Hessians) – Obstlt Kurt v. Dalwigk-Schauenburg
100 horse
Franz v. Dalwigk (Hessians) – Oberst Franz Elgar v. Dalwigk
50 horse
Thilo Albrecht v. Uslar's (Hessians) [5] – Rittmeister Birkenfeld
50 horse
Beckermann's Horse Regt – Oberst Eberhard Beckermann
4 coys, 150 horse
Bulach's Horse Regt – Oberst Claus Conrad Zorn v. Bulach
8 coys, 120 horse
Goldstein's Horse Regt – Obstlt Marx Conrad v. Rehlinger [6]
8 coys, 150 horse
Duke Wilhelm of Sachsen-Weimar's Horse Regt
12 coys, 120 horse

INFANTRY CENTRE

Front line
Generalmajor Nils Brahe, Greve till Visingsborg

SWEDISH BRIGADE:
Obstlt Gabriel Kyle (1,581)
Erik Hand's (Swedish) Regt – Obstlt Gabriel Kyle [7]
(8) coys, 465 m, 267 p, 96 offs
Karl Hård's (Västergotland) Regt 8 coys, 447 m, 0 p, 96 offs
*Klas Hastfer's (Finland) Regt [8] 4 coys, 156 m, 0 p, 48 offs

YELLOW (GUARDS) BRIGADE:
GenMaj Nils Brahe (1,221)
King's Lifeguard – KptLt Erik Stenbock
1 coy, 45 m, 38 p, 12 offs
Yellow or Hof (Court) Regt – GenMaj Nils Brahe
16 coys, 610 m, 324 p, 192 offs

BLUE BRIGADE:
Oberst Hans Georg aus dem Winckel (1,110)
Winckel's 'Old Blue' Regt 16 coys, 486 m, 432 p, 192 offs

DUKE BERNHARD'S (GREEN) BRIGADE:
Oberst Georg Wulf v. Wildenstein (2,036)
Duke Bernhard's (Green) Leibregiment [7] – Obstlt Johann Winckler
12 coys, 396 m, 210 p, 142 offs
Wildenstein's Regt – Oberst Georg Wulf v. Wildenstein
12 coys, 468 m, 102 p, 142 offs
Leslie's Scots Regt – Obstlt Ludovick Leslie
16 coys, 360 m, 24 p, 192 offs

FRONT LINE RESERVE: (228)
Henderson's Regt [10] – Oberst John Henderson
4 coys, 180 m, 0 p, 48 offs

Rear line
'Generalmajor of the Army' Dodo v. Knyphausen

DUKE WILHELM'S BRIGADE: [11]
Oberst Carl Bose (1,996 of which 1,726 at Lützen)
Wilhelm of Weimar's Leibregt – Obstlt Georg Philip v. Zehm
12 coys, 276 m, 78 p, 142 offs
Carl Bose's (Saxon) Regt 8 coys, 540 m, 156 p, 96 offs
Pforte's (Saxon) Regt – Oberst Hans von der Pforte
4 coys, 306 m, 84 p, 48 offs
[Detached to guard the camp at Naumburg:
Dam Vitzthum's (Saxon) Regt – Oberst Damien v. Vitzthum-Eckstädt
8 coys, 150 m, 24 p, 96 offs]

KNYPHAUSEN'S BRIGADE:
GenMaj Dodo v. Knyphausen (1,120)
Knyphausen's (White) Regt [12], 12 coys: 708 m, 270 p, 142 offs

THURN'S BRIGADE:
Oberst Hans Jakob Graf v. Thurn (1,832)
Thurn's (Black) Regt 8 coys, 240 m, 144 p, 96 offs
Isenburg's Regt – Oberst Wolfgang Heinrich Graf v. Isenburg-Büdingen; probably under Obstlt Detlof v. Bellin
8 coys, 120 m, 54 p, 96 offs

Landgraf Wilhelm of Hessen-Kassel's Green Leibregiment
Oberst Caspar Graf Eberstein;
under Obstlt Hans Heinrich v Güntherode
12 coys, 216 m, 144 p, 142 offs
*Erbach's Regt – Oberst Georg Friedrich Graf v. Erbach (Erpach) [13];
under his oberstleutnant. 8 coys, 144 m, 18 p, 96 offs

*Thilo Albrecht v. Uslar's (Hessian) Regt
Obstlt Alexander v. Östringer. 12 coys, 144 m, 36 p, 142 offs

MITZLAFF'S BRIGADE:
Oberst Joachim Mitzlaff (1,834)
Gersdorf's Regt [14]
8 coys, 330 m, 96 p, 96 offs
Mitzlaff's Regt
12 coys, 342 m, 198 p, 142 offs
Rossow's Regt – Oberst Friedrich v. Rossow/Rosen/Rosa
8 coys, 366 m, 168 p, 96 offs

REAR LINE RESERVE:
Öhm's Horse Regt – Oberst Johann Bernhard v. Öhm
8 coys, 300 horse

LEFT WING
Bernhard, Duke of Sachsen-Weimar

Front line
Bernhard, Duke of Sachsen-Weimar

Duke Bernhard of Weimar's Leibregiment – Obstlt Bouillon
12 coys, 500 horse, deployed as two squadrons.
Carberg's Horse Regt – Oberst Carl Joachim Carberg
8 coys, 220 horse
Kurland Horse – Oberst Hans? Wrangel. 4 coys, 230 horse
Livonian Horse – Obstlt Karl? v. Tiesenhausen. 8 coys, 300 horse
Courville's Horse Regt – Oberst Nicholas de Courville
5 coys, 300 horse

Commanded musketeers – Oberst Gersdorf [15]
5 bodies each of c.200 men with two 3-pdr regimental guns

Rear line [16]
Oberst Ernst, Duke of Sachsen-Weimar [17]

Hofkirchen's Regt (Saxons) – GM Lorentz v Hofkirchen; under his oberstleutnant. [18] 12 coys, 350 horse
Prince Ernst of Anhalt's Regt (Saxons) – Ernst, Prince of Anhalt-Bernburg. 8 coys, 300 horse
Löwenstein's Horse Regt – Oberst Georg Ludwig Graf v. Löwenstein; commanded by its major. 6 coys, 200 horse
Brandenstein's Horse Regt – Oberst Brandenstein [19]
4 coys, 300 horse
Steinbach's Regt, – Oberst Jaroslav Wolf v. Steinbach
4 coys, 200 horse
Stechnitz – Obstlt Georg Matthias v. Stechnitz (Tiechenitz)
4 coys, 80 horse (including remnants of Jean de Hontas de Gassion's French coy)
Field Artillery – Major Joen Persson Jernlod [20]
20 guns, mostly 12- and 24-pdrs

Other troops
Deployed as commanded musketeers 'interlined' among the cavalry:
Brandenstein Inf Regt – Oberst Brandenstein
4 coys, 198m, 0p, 48offs
Löwenstein's Inf Regt – Oberst Georg Ludwig Graf v. Löwenstein
7 coys, 600m, 0p, 84 offs

Detached, probably guarding lines of communication:
Dragoons – from the regiments/companies of GenMaj Georg Christoph v. Taupadel, Obstlt Ambrosius and Obstlt Pierre Margalli
600 mounted infantry

Key: m = musketeers, p = pikemen, off = officers, v. = von

The three infantry units marked with an asterisk (*) were not mentioned in the (incomplete) casualty lists, and may have been detached.

Notes to Swedish order of battle

Main source: Army clerk Tönnes Hindersson Langman's list of the Swedish Army on 14 November 1632, before the march from Naumburg (*Historiskt Tidskrift*, 1892, s.159+). For cavalry regiments all figures are 'effective' mounted field strengths including officers. Infantry regiments are always listed with a full complement of officers; actual strengths were almost certainly lower.

1 Duke Wilhelm of Weimar was absent claiming ill-health and had temporarily entrusted his post to his younger brother, Duke Bernhard, whose official rank was Generalmajor of Horse.
2 Eberstein had his own infantry regiment, which fought in Thurn's Brigade. The 'commanded musketeers' came mainly from Brandenstein's and Löwenstein's regiments.
3 The Swedish General Staff refer to Bulach as Generalmajor, a rank he seems to have obtained shortly after Lützen.
4 *The Swedish Intelligencer*, 3, p.168 notes that Georg v. Uslar was 'a Sergeant-Major General: though now he commanded his owne men onely'. He is perhaps confused with his brother, the Hessian Generalmajor Thilo Albrecht, who had two regiments at Lützen, but was not himself present. Swedish records refer to Georg as oberst.
5 Thilo Albrecht v. Uslar's Horse were also known as Landgraf Wilhelm's Lifeguard.
6 GenLt-of-Horse Wilhelm v. Goldstein was terminally ill; his regiment had been combined with Rehlinger's after Alte Feste.
7 Oberst Erik Hand was mortally wounded at Alte Feste and died in captivity. His successor had yet to be promoted. The regiment (sometimes called the New Blue regiment) was a composite of several national regiments, the core of which was Hand's Östergötland regiment.

8 Oberst Hastfer was not present at Lützen. Four companies of his Finnish regiment remained in garrison at Königshofen near Nuremberg.
9 Not to be confused with Hepburn's Green Regiment, which had passed to Adam v. Pfuel. Bernhard's Regiment, like Hepburn's, was mostly German.
10 Henderson's regiment may have been a dragoon unit he had raised for Duke Wilhelm of Weimar, which had failed to obtain horses.
11 *Sveriges Krig* calls this Bose's Brigade. Contemporaries described it as Duke Wilhelm's Brigade even though Duke Wilhelm was not at the battle.
12 Knyphausen received the White Regiment after the death of its colonel, Wilhelm Burt, soon after Alte Feste; the unit was strengthened in October 1632 by the incorporation of Mitschefall's Regiment.
13 Erbach had been wounded at Alte Feste, some sources say fatally.
14 During the battle Oberst Gersdorf led the 'commanded musketeer' bodies accompanying the Swedish left-wing cavalry.
15 The commanded musketeers were drawn out of Löwenstein's and Brandenstein's regiments. Monro (who was not at the battle) states that Leslie's Scots also supplied command men on this wing.
16 The Protestant sketch of the battle (p.52) shows a different arrangement of the rear line, with from left to right: Brandenstein, Hertzog Ernst [of Weimar]. 3 cornets [Stechnitz?], Steinbach, [Prince Ernst of] Anhalt, and Hofkirch.
17 *The Swedish Intelligencer* lists Prince Ernst of Anhalt as commander of the rear line. It is more likely that Bernhard's elder brother Duke Ernst had this honour.
18 Lorentz v. Hofkirchen was absent from his unit commanding Saxon troops, so could never have met his brother Albrecht, commander of Sparr's Imperial regiment, at Lützen.
19 There were two Colonel Brandensteins in Swedish service, Georg Friedrich and the infamous Count Christof Karl. It has not been possible to establish which of them commanded the Lützen regiments.
20 The colonel of the artillery, Lennart Torstensson, had been captured at Alte Feste.

WALLENSTEIN'S ARMY

North European historians have habitually portrayed Wallenstein's army as a raw, untried force, hastily assembled in early 1632 to replace Tilly's devastated legions and incapable of matching Gustav Adolf's veterans. In fact, many of Wallenstein's regiments had longer traditions than Sweden's Colour regiments. At least three of the units present at Lützen were raised in the 1610s, and many more in the 1620s; several had even faced the Swedes before, as part of a corps sent to help Poland in 1629.

Wallenstein's forces were even more diverse than Gustav Adolf's. Recruited throughout Catholic Europe, they included Germans, Austrians, Czechs, Italians, Hungarians, Poles and Croatians. Italian officers were (like Gustav Adolf's Scots) highly valued. (Ordinary Italian soldiers were notoriously unreliable in the northern winter, and the men of Piccolomini's horse and Colloredo's foot regiments were mostly Germans.) Pappenheim's army included several regiments of Walloons (French-speaking Belgians), famed for their ferocity.

The **Imperial cavalry** was organised into four main branches: cuirassiers, harquebusiers, dragoons and Croats. The ideal **cuirassier** was armed in three-quarter armour, blackened to prevent rust. By 1632 few except officers wore these costly and uncomfortable suits. Most cuirassiers were now what Montecuccoli called 'half cuirassiers', wearing only breast and back plate, and open-faced helmet. The cuirassier's main weapons were a sword and a pair of pistols, intended for close combat rather than 'caracoling'.

Harquebusiers rode smaller horses and had little armour: most made do with a buffcoat. Named after their long arquebuses (carbines), they were intended for campaign duties and skirmishes, to save the cuirassiers for serious action. In reality the distinction between cuirassiers and harquebusiers was blurring. Many regiments were raised as harquebusiers and upgraded to cuirassiers when they acquired better equipment and horses. Piccolomini's famous regiment was still officially a harquebusier unit, yet was better armoured than many cuirassier regiments.

Cartridges had been in use as early as the 15th century to speed the firing of cannon. Swedish regimental guns employed cartridges of the type shown here, with balls fastened to the powder charge and wooden framework by wire, which according to the Swedish military engineer Schildknecht, allowed them to fire three shots to every two of the musketeers. It was a ball from a shot of this type that caused Pappenheim's fatal wound. (Livrustkammaren/Skokloster)

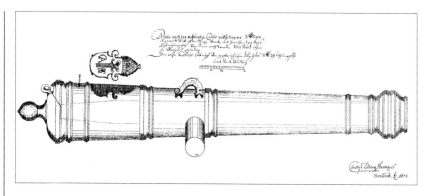

All the Imperial **dragoons** engaged at Lützen seem to have been raised during 1632. They are described in the official army lists as 'German horsemen, armed with half-armour (*halb Harnisch*, probably a breast plate) and equipped with firelocks (*Feuergewehr*)'. Though expected to carry out menial duties like their Swedish counterparts, they were listed as part of the cavalry rather than the infantry, and occasionally (as at Lützen) fought mounted.

Croats or Crabats were described in the official Imperial army lists as 'light horse armed in the Hungarian manner'. Most commanders of Croat regiments were Hungarians, as were many troopers, who were recruited from both Slav and Magyar provinces of the Habsburg realm. Croats were of little value in a stand-up fight; armed with carbines as their primary weapon, their duties were off-battlefield – skirmishing, patrolling and making campaign life unpleasant for the enemy, a task they carried out with admirabl diligence during Gustav Adolf's long, wasted summer at Nuremberg. In battle, they were deployed on the wings of the army, attempting to turn the enemy flanks, distracting units that might be better employed by the enemy elsewhere. In their fur hats and long eastern coats, they made a colourful if unpredictable addition to the Imperial ranks. The irregular horse also included small units described as Hungarian or Polish. These are listed almost interchangeably with the Croats, but had distinctive dress or weaponry. The three companies of 'Polish Cossacks' present at Lützen were recruited inside the Polish realm and should not be confused with the Cossacks of the Russian Steppes.

The **Imperial infantry** tended to be more heavily armoured than their Swedish opponents. Austrian and south German styles of pikeman's armour did exist, but as Wallenstein purchased much of his equipment via Nuremberg, his infantry probably differed little in appearance from their Swedish counterparts. Imperial infantry regiments had a standard organisation of ten companies, each of 200 men. However few units could maintain even half this strength in the field. Nevertheless Imperial regiments were stronger, on average, than Swedish regiments. In battle they formed up in 1,000-strong battalions (often called 'brigades', because several weak regiments would combine to make up a single battalion). Montecuccoli notes that at Lützen Wallenstein drew up his infantry seven deep, as a result of his idiosyncratic desire to position the company colours at the exact centre of the pike blocks!

The **Imperial artillery** had some of the most beautiful cannon in Europe. By 1632 they were being manufactured in standardised calibres:

Most successful of Gustav Adolf's technological innovations were his regimental cannon. These brass field pieces, firing an iron ball of 3–4 pounds (1.5–2 kg) weight, were a huge advance on the famous 'leather cannon', which had been left behind in Polish Prussia or returned to Stockholm before the German campaign. Crewed by two men, they were able to advance at the same pace as the infantry. During the battle half of the 40 regimental cannon available were given out to the infantry brigades, the other half were attached in pairs to the 'sleeves' of commanded musketeers on the cavalry wings.

demi-cannon (24-pdrs), quarter-cannon (12-pdrs) and eighth-cannon (6-pdrs). A number of older pieces remained in use, and for example we hear of 'quarter-cannon' of 10, 12, 14 and 16 pounds calibre, captured by the Swedes at Lützen, or shortly thereafter.

The Imperial and Catholic League armies were already employing regimental cannon in 1631, although in smaller numbers than the Swedes. Wallenstein's army instructions of 4 May 1632 imply that many units possessed them and there are occasional references during the Lützen campaign. Two guns per Imperial regiment became the standard allocation from 1633, and may have been the case earlier. About two guns per front-line infantry battalion would have been the minimum available at Lützen.

IMPERIAL ORDER OF BATTLE

Generalissimus (Oberst-Kapitän) Albrecht Wentzel Eusebius v. Waldstejn, Duke of Friedland and Mecklenburg

Second-in-command
Feldmarschall-leutnant Heinrich Holk

Third-in-command
Generalwachtmeister Rudolf Freiherr v. Colloredo-Mels, Graf v. Waldsee

Infantry Regiments
Baden – Inhaber: Oberst Wilhelm, Markgraf of Baden-Baden; under Obstlt Stopler. 6 coys, 500 men, raised 1630
Friedrich Breuner – Oberst Philipp Friedrich v. Breuner
  10 coys, 500 men, raised 1632
GenFZM Breuner – GenFZM Hans Philipp v. Breuner
  13 coys, c.900 men, raised 1618
Alt-Breuner – Oberst Hans Gottfried v. Breuner
  5 coys, c.500 men, raised 1630
Colloredo – GenWm Rudolf v. Colloredo; under Obstlt Philipp Hussmann de Namedi. 7 coys, c.700 men, raised 1625
Comargo (Leaguist)– Oberst Theodor Comargo
  10 coys, c.800 men, raised 1619
Grana – Oberst Francesco Grana, Marchese di Caretto
  8 coys, c.1,000 men, raised 1627
Kehraus – Oberst Andreas Matthias Kehraus
  10 coys, c.1,200 men, raised 1618
Reinach (Leaguist, detachment),[21] c.150 men, raised 1620
Alt-Sachsen – Inhaber: Heinrich Julius Herzog zu Sachsen-Lauenburg; under Obstlt Bernard Hemmerle
    8 coys, 800 men, raised 1618
Waldstein – Oberst Berthold v. Waldstein
  11 coys, c.1,500 men, raised 1628

Cuirassier Regiments
Desfours – Oberst Nicolas Desfours
  6 coys, c.300 horse, raised 1628
Götz [22] – Inhaber: Oberst Johann v. Götz;
under Obstlt Moritz v. Falkenberg. 9 coys, c.400 men, raised 1626
Holk – Obstlt Frantz v. Uhlefeld or Obstlt Tiesenhausen
  8 coys, 250 men, raised 1630
Lohe [23] – Oberst von der Lohe
  5 coys, 150 men, raised 1632
Alt-Trčka [24] – Oberst Adam Erdmann Graf v. Trčka (Terzky)
  4 coys, c.250 horse, raised 1629

Harquebusier Regiments
Drost [25] – Oberst Wilhelm v. Westfalen, Landdrost von Dringenberg
  5 coys, 250 horse, raised 1632
Goschütz – Oberst Benedikt Goschütz (Goschitzki)
  5 coys, c.250 horse, raised 1632
Hagen – Oberst Johann Nicolaus Hagen v. Sauwenbein
  13 coys, c.800 horse, raised 1631 and 1632
Leutersheim – Oberst Johann Freiherr v. Leutersheim (Leittersam)
  6 coys, c.200 horse, raised 1632
Loyers – Oberst Gottfried Freiherr v. Loyers
  5 coys, c.200 horse, raised 1632
Piccolomini – Oberst Ottavio Piccolomini di Aragona
  12 coys,[26] c.500 horse, raised 1629
Westfalen – Oberst Heinrich Leo v. Westfalen
  3 coys (part regiment), c.150 horse, raised 1632
Westrumb – Oberst Johann v. Westrumb (Westrem)
  3 coys, c.100 horse, raised 1632

Dragoon Regiments
Trčka – Inhaber: Oberst Adam Graf v. Trčka
  5 coys, c.100 men, raised 1632

Croat Regiments
Isolano – General Ludwig Johann Hector Graf v. Isolano
    5 coys, 250 horse, raised 1625–32
Beygott – Oberst Daniel Beygott. 5 coys, 100 horse, raised 1632
Corpes – Oberst Marcus Corpes. 10 coys, 300 horse, raised 1631
Révay – Oberst Paul Freiherr von Révay
  5 coys, 250, horse 1632

Artillery
General-feldzeugmeister Hans Philipp v. Breuner
19–21 cannon, incl. nine 24-pdrs, six 12-pdrs and four 6-pdrs.
Regimental cannon
Two per infantry regiment in theory, fewer in reality.

Feldmarschall Gottfried Heinrich Graf v. Pappenheim

Second-in-command[28]
Generalwachtmeister Heinrich Graf Reinach

Cavalry Regiments

Bönninghausen's Harquebusier Regt – Oberst Löthar
v. Bönninghausen
  11 coys, c.500 men, raised 1630

Bredau's Cuirassier Regt – Oberst Hans Rudolf v. Bredau
  6 coys, c.300 men, raised 1631

Lamboy's Harquebusier Regt – Oberst Wilhelm v. Lamboy
  6–8 coys, c.250 men, raised 1632

Sparr's Cuirassier Regt – Oberst Ernest Georg v. Sparr;
under Obstlt Albrecht v. Hofkirchen
  10 coys, c.300 men, raised 1629

Tontinelli's (ex-Lindelo's)[29] (Leaguist) Horse Regt
Obstlt Anton Tontinelli
  6 coys, c.250 horse, raised 1619

Dragoon & Guard units

Merode's Dragoon Regt (Walloons) – Inhaber: Oberst Jean Graf
Merode-Varoux; under Obstlt Robert Borneval d'Arlin
  4 coys, c.120 men, raised 1625 & 1632

Merode's 'Obwacht' Lifeguard
  1 coy, c.40 men

Pappenheim's Dragoons 3 coys, c.100 men, raised 1632?

Pappenheim's Rennfahne Lifeguard [30] 1 coy, c.40 men

Irregular light horse

Batthyanyi's Croats – Oberst Franz Graf Batthyanyi
  9 coys, c.200 horse, raised 1632

Forgacs's Croats – Oberst Nicolas Forgacs (Forgatsch) de Gymes
  2 coys, c.100 horse, raised 1630

Orossy's Croats – Oberst Paulus Orossy (called 'Horatius')
  9 coys, c.450 horse, raised 1631

Polish Cossacks [31] 3 coys, c.250 horse, raised 1631 or 1632

Infantry regiments

Gil de Haes (Walloons) – Oberst Gil (Wilhelm) de Haes
  6 coys, c.500 men, raised 1632

Goltz – Oberst Martin Maximilian Freiherr von der Goltz
  10 coys, c.700 men, raised 1626

Moriamez-Pallant (Walloons) – Oberst Karl Dietrich Pallant,
Baron de Moriamez (Morialmé),
  8 coys, c.500 men, raised 1632

Pallant (Walloons) – Oberst Rudolf Freiherr v. Pallant
  10 coys, c.500 men, raised 1632

Reinach (Leaguist) (main body) – Obstlt Gabriel Freiherr Comargo
  10 coys, c.650 men, raised 1620

'Würzburg' Regt (Leaguist) (remnants) [32] – Hauptmann Willich
  c.75 men, raised 1631

Artillery

6 field guns, plus 1–2 regimental cannon per infantry regiment.

MAIN DETACHED UNITS

Detached to Eilenburg

Oberst Melchior von Hatzfeld

Hatzfeld's (ex-Neu-Sachsen) Cuirassier Regt
  6 coys, 600 horse, raised 1625

Mansfeld's Infantry Regiment – Inhaber: Graf Philip v. Mansfeld;
under Obstlt Niderum
  10? coys, c.500 men, raised 1625

Thun's (ex-Traun) Infantry Regiment – Oberst Rudolf Thun
  7 coys (part regiment), c.600 men, raised 1631

Trčka's Infantry Regt – Inhaber: Oberst Adam Graf Trčka; under
Obstlt Adrian Enckhevoert. 7 coys, c.800 men, raised 1631

Detached to Altenburg, then Chemnitz

Contreras's Infantry Regiment – Oberst Andreas v. Contreras
  5 coys, c.400 men, raised 1628

Detached to Zwickau

De Suys' (Walloon) Infantry Regiment – Oberst Ernest Roland
Baron de Suys
  10 coys, c.700 men, raised 1631

Notes to Imperial order of battle

Imperial unit strengths are all highly speculative. Imperial commanders kept
records of numbers of companies rather than men, and often exaggerated to
mislead the enemy. The commanded musketeers deployed in Lützen town and
the roadside ditches were drawn out of the infantry regiments, so regimental
and brigade strengths need not match.

21 According to Holk's orders of 14 November, 300 men from Comargo's and
    Reinach's regiments were to garrison Weissenfels; the Reinach detachment
    would have fought as part of Comargo's brigade.
22 In late 1632 Götz sold his regiment to the Emperor's 19-year-old nephew
    Mattias de' Medici, Duke of Florence; it is not clear if this transaction was
    completed before Lützen.
23 In September 1632 Lohe's newly raised cuirassiers were described as
    'ill-clad', suggesting few had armour.
24 Trčka owned two cuirassier regiments. The newer one (Neu-Trčka), raised
    in 1631, was in Bohemia. *Sveriges Krig* gives Alt-Trčka 12 companies
    and 800 men, which probably includes the strength of Trčka's
    closely-associated dragoon regiment.
25 Drost was short for the civil title 'Landdrost'. The regiment is often confused
    with Heinrich Leo v. Westfalen's many units.
26 Includes two companies of Wallenstein's former bodyguard. A new
    two-company harquebusier bodyguard appears in the records from early
    1633 under Obstlt. Tornetta.
27 The term 'corps' (actually corpus – Latin for body) appears in the Imperial
    army lists from late 1632.
28 Officially second in command of Pappenheim's corps was Jean Graf
    Merode-Vâroux. He received a gift of 1,000 ducâts from Wallenstein after
    Lützen, but it is unclear if he was personally present.
29 The remnants of General Thimon von Lindelo's Leaguist regiment, rebuilt
    over summer 1632 by Pappenheim, and later taken into Imperial service by
    Wallenstein.
30 Stadler believes that Pappenheim's Rennfahne was part of his dragoon unit,
    but this is not conclusively proven.
31 The Poles seem to have been recruited privately, perhaps by the Silesian
    generalmajor Hans Ulrich Schaffgotsche.
32 A regiment raised by the Bishop of Würzburg, the colonel of which is
    disputed.

Field-signs

Because the equipment of the rival armies differed only in subtle details, the opponents employed another means of distinguishing themselves in the field. During the 1631 campaign both sides used only improvised field-signs – sprigs of green foliage worn in the headgear by Gustav Adolf's troops, and white strips of cloth tied round arm or hat among Tilly's veterans. Determined to systematise the practice Wallenstein in May 1632 had ordered the use of red scarves (sashes) in his army and forbade the wearing of all other colours under pain of death. There is little evidence that Gustav Adolf adopted a single scarf colour: his officers seem to have worn any colour they liked, except, of course, red.

Since most infantrymen were never issued scarves, as important a form of identification was the 'field-word'– both a password and a battle cry, issued afresh for each battle. Not one to break with convention Wallenstein chose the stock Catholic field-word: *Jesus, Maria!* Meanwhile Gustav Adolf stuck with the phrase that had brought him luck at Breitenfeld: *Gott mit uns!* (God with us).

OPPOSING PLANS

Wallenstein's goals

After Nuremberg, Wallenstein turned his attention towards Saxony, a reluctant but crucial ally of Sweden. Wallenstein was well acquainted with the character of the Saxon Elector, Duke Johann Georg: weak, vain and an alcoholic, he was incapable of leading the Protestant cause and was jealous of Gustav Adolf's fame. Wallenstein believed it would take little to detach him from the Swedish alliance, and, as he explained to Pappenheim, 'if the Elector is lost, the King must be lost too'.

The main Saxon army under Hans Georg von Arnim (or Arnheim) was absent in Silesia, and a small Imperial diversionary force sent into Saxony under Feldmarschal-leutnant Heinrich Holk had spectacular success. Cutting a swathe of destruction everywhere he passed Holk penetrated deep into Vogtland and Meissen, as far as the suburbs of the Saxon capital, Dresden. Reinforcing success, Wallenstein decided to make for Saxony with the rest of his army. With the campaign season drawing in, Saxony, still relatively unspoilt by war, also promised attractive winter quarters for his troops. He was encouraged by his astrologer, Seni, who had advised him that November would bring a change in the fortunes of the Swedish King.

Wallenstein at first planned to march directly on Dresden. After rejoining Holk in mid-October, he was persuaded to first seize Saxony's second city, Leipzig. After taking the key bridges on the Elbe and the Saale, Wallenstein could effectively seal off most of Saxony and reduce it at leisure.

The subjection of Saxony required a concentration of Imperial forces. Pappenheim had for much of 1632 been running his own highly successful war in the Lower Saxon Circle of north-west Germany, and ignored Wallenstein's urgings to join him. It was only a direct order from the Emperor that pushed him to obey. Setting off from Hildesheim, Pappenheim marched rapidly south and was near Erfurt, the leading city of Thuringia, by 28 October, where he demanded a 20,000-thaler ransom. Pappenheim's instructions were to reduce the territory on the west bank of the Saale. If he could also

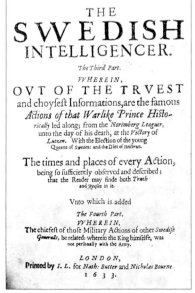

THE
SWEDISH
INTELLIGENCER.

The Third Part.

WHEREIN,

OVT OF THE TRVEST
and choysest Informations, are the famous
Actions of that Warlike Prince Histo-
rically led along; from the *Norimberg Leaguer,*
unto the day of his death, at the *Victory of*
Lutzen. With the Election of the young
Queene of *Sweden:* and the Diet of *Heilbrun.*

The times and places of every Action,
being so sufficiently observed and described;
that the Reader may finde both *Truth*
and *Reason* in it.

Vnto which is added

The Fourth Part.
WHEREIN,
The chiefest of those Military Actions of other *Swedish*
Generals, be related: wherein the King himselfe, was
not personally with the Army.

LONDON,
Printed by *I. L.* for *Nath: Butter* and *Nicholas Bourne.*
1 6 3 3.

The Swedish Intelligencer, published in London from 1632, was the main English-language source on Gustav Adolf's campaigns. The author was Dr William Watts, future chaplain to Prince Rupert, who had travelled widely in Germany. His main sources for the Lützen campaign were two British officers, LtCol Francis Tyrwhitt (Terret) and Cpt. Edward Feilding, formerly of the Marquis of Hamilton's army, who were captured by Croats near Weissenfels on 11 November and spent the battle as prisoners among Wallenstein's baggage train.

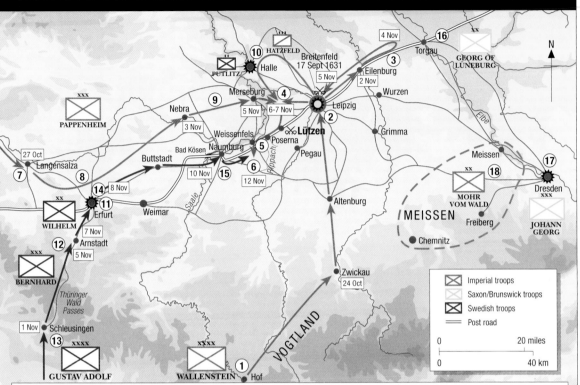

OPERATIONS IN SAXONY 21 OCT – 12 NOV 1632
SHOWING THE MOVEMENTS OF THE RIVAL ARMIES LEADING UP TO THE BATTLE OF LÜTZEN

1. Mid-October: Wallenstein, with c.18,000 men, meets Holk at Hof, who persuades him to abandon his original plan of marching on Dresden, and instead to seize Leipzig.
2. 28 October: Wallenstein lays siege to Leipzig, which falls on 1 November Leipzig's Pleissenburg castle surrenders on 2 November.
3. Wallenstein marches to seize the Elbe bridge at Torgau, but on reaching Eilenburg (4 November) receives news that Gustav Adolf is at Erfurt, and so turns back for Leipzig.
4. 6-7 November: Pappenheim's army joins Wallenstein's on the plain east of Merseburg.
5. 10-11 November: Wallenstein quarters the Imperial army in and around Weissenfels.
6. 12 November: Wallenstein's and Pappenheim's combined armies in battle array confront Gustav Adolf south of Weissenfels. Feeling himself too weak in horse, the Swedish king retires and begins to fortify the camp at Naumburg.
7. Recalled from the Weser/Lower Saxony region on the emperor's order, Pappenheim with about 6,000 men marches south-east for joint operations with Wallenstein, his mission being to reduce Saxony area

west of the Saale. After entering Mühlhausen on 26 October, he loots Langensalza on 27 October.
8. Pappenheim demands 20,000 reichsthalers ransom from Erfurt.
9. On hearing that the main Swedish army is marching north, Pappenheim heads east to join Wallenstein, passing through Nebra on 3 November, and crossing the Saale at Merseburg on 5 November.
10. A cavalry regiment from Wallenstein's army under Oberst Hatzfeld fails to take Halle, which is garrisoned by 150 Swedish troops under Oberstleutnant Putlitz. Hatzfeld is recalled to the main Imperial army on 6 November.
11. On hearing of Pappenheim's approach Duke Wilhelm of Sachsen-Weimar, second-in-command of Swedish forces in Germany, concentrates locally available forces (about 3,000 men) at Erfurt.
12. Bernhard of Sachsen-Weimar, operating independently of Gustav Adolf since mid-September with about 7,000 men, hurries north from Franconia to secure the Thüringer Wald passes before Pappenheim can close them. He reaches Arnstadt on 31 October.
13. Gustav Adolf forced-marches north from Swabia via

Nuremberg covering over 600 km in 17 days. He personally enters Arnstadt on 2 November, his slower troops follow and combine with Bernhard's army between 5 and 7 November.
14. The combined Swedish army reaches Erfurt, and receives further reinforcement from Duke Wilhelm of Weimar's detachments.
15. 8 November: Brandenstein with the Swedish advance guard, seizes the Salle bridge at Bad Kösen and, finding only token resistence, enters Naumburg. 10 November: Gustav Adolf with the main army enters Naumburg and camps south of the town.
16. 4,000 Saxon troops and 2,000 Brunswick-Lüneburg cavalry, block the Elbe bridge at Torgau. Gustav Adolf's order for the Lüneburg horse to hurry to his aid are countermanded by the Saxon C-in-C Hans Georg v. Arnim.
17. Duke Johann Georg remains in the Saxon capital Dresden with 6,000 Saxon garrison troops.
18. Mohr vom Wald is quartered in the Meissen region with the responsibility of watching Johann Georg's Saxons in Dresden and maintaining contact with Gallas in Bohemia.

close the passes over the Thüringer Wald, no amount of Swedish troops would be able to prevent Wallenstein's plan for the conquest of Saxony.

Gustav Adolf's goals

The wasted summer at Nuremberg had been a blow to Gustav Adolf's prestige. But six weeks on, and a whirlwind campaign through Bavaria, Swabia, Upper Pfalz and Franconia had restored confidence in the Protestant ranks. Swedish field armies in other parts of Germany were also flush with success, and it seemed that every report that arrived in the Swedish headquarters brought word of another Protestant victory.

News that Wallenstein had invaded Saxony came as a surprise to the Swedish King. The danger to Erfurt, at the centre of the German road network, could not be ignored since it threatened communications with Sweden and the newly captured Baltic shoreline of Germany. Gustav Adolf had to act fast.

After Nuremberg Duke Bernhard had separated from the main Swedish army to conduct independent operations in Franconia. For the campaign in Saxony, he was ordered to hurry to Erfurt, where he was to rejoin the King. Bernhard successfully crossed the Thüringian passes before Pappenheim was able to close them and then waited for Gustav Adolf.

As Gustav Adolf marched north at a whirlwind pace, he saw the late autumn campaign in Saxony as an opportunity to finally catch Wallenstein and finish the whole business once and for good.

INITIAL CONTACTS

Duke Ernst of Sachsen-Weimar (1601–74), nicknamed 'the Pious', was regarded as one of the noblest princes of Germany. He caught pneumonia after swimming the Lech during the battle at Rain, but returned to health in time to fight at Lützen, where according to Watts he commanded his elder brother Duke Wilhelm of Weimar's cavalry regiment. However, the Protestant sketch of the battle shows him on the opposite wing commanding a cavalry unit of his own and it is likely that he had control of the whole of the left-wing reserve cavalry.

When Wallenstein heard news that Gustav Adolf was concentrating near Erfurt, his plans needed revision. Leipzig castle had fallen on 2 November and Wallenstein was then on his way to Torgau, hoping to seize the Elbe bridge that would finally seal off Saxony from the east. Now there was a more urgent task – the Swede could not be allowed to operate behind his back, and had to be prevented from crossing the Saale into Saxony.

Wallenstein immediately called off the advance on Torgau and ordered Pappenheim east to join him. Crossing the Saale at Merseburg, Pappenheim came personally to meet Wallenstein at Wurzen on 7 November. Meanwhile the two Imperial armies combined on the plain between Merseburg and Leipzig, and all officers were ordered to rejoin the ranks under pain of death.

Also on 7 November, the concentration of Protestant forces near Erfurt was completed. The King had covered 600km in just 17 days, and now spared a few moments for his wife. It was hardly an intimate event: he dined in his chambers with her and with Duke Ernst of Weimar, but was constantly interrupted by mail and intelligence reports. Early next morning he bade her farewell for the last time and rejoined the army, which had already began its march.

Later on 8 November an advance party of about 100 men under Oberst Brandenstein found the main bridge over the Saale poorly guarded and captured Naumburg only hours before two Imperial regiments, De Suys' foot and Bredau's cuirassiers, arrived on the scene. The main body with the King followed on 10 November to a rapturous reception, the citizens of Naumburg crowding the streets to touch Gustav Adolf's clothes. The religious overtones deeply embarrassed the King, who confided to his chaplain, Dr Jacob Fabricius: 'Everyone venerates me so, and treats me as some sort of god … The Lord will soon punish me for this.'

By this time Wallenstein had shifted his HQ to Weissenfels and the patrols of both armies were very close. On 12 November Gustav Adolf made a reconnaissance with most of his cavalry towards Weissenfels, only to find Wallenstein drawn up in full battle order on the plain south of the town. Combined with Pappenheim's corps, the Imperial army was an awe-inspiring sight, especially the cavalry, which was superior in numbers and quality to the Swedish horse. The King contemplated whether to risk battle.

Gustav Adolf knew that his ally, Duke Georg of Brunswick-Lüneburg, had 2,000 Protestant horse at Torgau – enough to swing a battle in his favour. He wrote, ordering Duke Georg to send the cavalry immediately towards Naumburg. To confuse Wallenstein, the King began to fortify his temporary lager at Naumburg – 'which was merely contrived to make the enemy feel secure in his quarters', wrote the Swedish correspondent Hallenus. Wallenstein's reaction came as a genuine surprise.

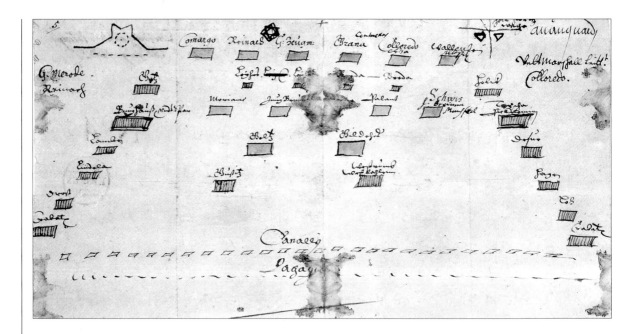

Wallenstein disperses his army, 14 November

Wallenstein convened a staff conference at his quarters in the Weissenfels inn *Zum Schützen*, on the afternoon of 13 November.[1] The result was a dramatic turnaround in the Imperial game-plan: Wallenstein decided to retreat from Weissenfels and break up his army. This was not provoked, as is often claimed, by a desire to go into winter quarters.

Gustav Adolf's retreat from Weissenfels and his entrenchment work at Naumburg suggested that he did not have the nerve to fight an open battle. For his part Wallenstein could not take the battle to the Swedish King at Naumburg – the road from Weissenfels was narrow and cut through hilly terrain, making it hazardous to approach in battle order. But then Wallenstein could not remain where he was: the nights were unseasonably cold for November, and there was insufficient room in Weissenfels and the surrounding villages to shelter all of his troops.

At the same time Wallenstein had received alarming reports from other theatres in Germany. After several months' siege a Swedish army under Gustav Horn had captured the key fortress of Benfeld south of Strasbourg on 7 November: the Rhine was now as good as closed to the Spanish. Meanwhile, during Pappenheim's absence from Lower Saxony, the Protestants had been able to push south to threaten the seat of the Archbishop-Elector of Cologne. Immediate action was needed and Pappenheim demanded to be sent back to continue the job that he believed he should never have been summoned from in the first place. Plagued by his gout, Wallenstein did not have the strength to argue.

Pappenheim was allowed to leave, but was instructed, on his way, to take the castle in Halle which, garrisoned by the Swedish Oberstleutnant Putlitz with 150 soldiers, had stubbornly refused to admit Hatzfeld's cavalry a few days earlier. Wallenstein saw the risk of letting Pappenheim go, but already had a contingency plan. On 11 November he had sent orders to Gallas in Bohemia, ordering him to force-march his 6,600-strong corps to Saxony. After passing south of Dresden, Gallas was

Imperialist battle array, long believed to be a plan of the battle of Lützen. It dates, in fact, from 12 November and a battle that never quite happened south of Weissenfels. The same deployment was followed a few days later at Lützen, though many of the units were no longer present. (Heeres Museum, Vienna)

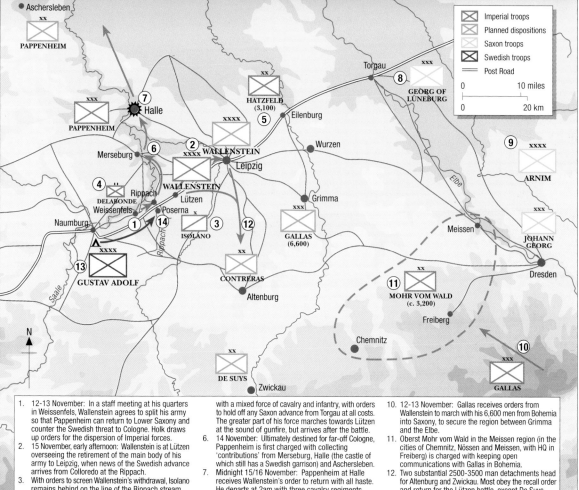

THE STRATEGIC SITUATION ON 15 NOVEMBER 1632
showing the dispersal of Imperial forces (planned and actual), at the time of Wallenstein's decision to recall the army to Lützen.

Legend:
- Imperial troops
- Planned dispositions
- Saxon troops
- Swedish troops
- Post Road

0 ——— 10 miles
0 ——— 20 km

Map labels: Aschersleben, PAPPENHEIM, PAPPENHEIM, Halle, Merseburg, HATZFELD (3,100), Eilenburg, Torgau, GEORG OF LÜNEBURG, Wurzen, WALLENSTEIN, WALLENSTEIN, Leipzig, ARNIM, Rippach, Lützen, Grimma, DELABONDE, Weissenfels, Poserna, Naumburg, ISOLANO, GALLAS (6,600), Meissen, JOHANN GEORG, GUSTAV ADOLF, CONTRERAS, Altenburg, MOHR VOM WALD (c. 3,200), Dresden, Freiberg, Chemnitz, DE SUYS, Zwickau, GALLAS

1. 12-13 November: In a staff meeting at his quarters in Weissenfels, Wallenstein agrees to split his army so that Pappenheim can return to Lower Saxony and counter the Swedish threat to Cologne. Holk draws up orders for the dispersion of Imperial forces.
2. 15 November, early afternoon: Wallenstein is at Lützen overseeing the retirement of the main body of his army to Leipzig, when news of the Swedish advance arrives from Colloredo at the Rippach.
3. With orders to screen Wallenstein's withdrawal, Isolano remains behind on the line of the Rippach stream, where he is further delayed by romantic adventures at the Rippach inn.
4. 15 November, 10am: While visiting the Weissenfels garrison, Generalwachtmeister Rudolf Colloredo spots the main Swedish army south of Weissenfels, marching towards the Rippach. He escorts the garrison under Hauptmann Delabonde back to the Rippach.
5. 14 November: Oberst Hatzfeld is sent to Eilenburg

with a mixed force of cavalry and infantry, with orders to hold off any Saxon advance from Torgau at all costs. The greater part of his force marches towards Lützen at the sound of gunfire, but arrives after the battle.
6. 14 November: Ultimately destined for far-off Cologne, Pappenheim is first charged with collecting 'contributions' from Merseburg, Halle (the castle of which still has a Swedish garrison) and Aschersleben.
7. Midnight 15/16 November: Pappenheim at Halle receives Wallenstein's order to return with all haste. He departs at 2am with three cavalry regiments, leaving Reinach with the infantry and artillery to set off at first light.
8. Although ordered by Gustav Adolf to come to his aid, the 2,000 Lüneburg cavalry remain in Torgau, forbidden from moving by Arnim.
9. General-leutnant Hans Georg v. Arnim with the main Saxon field army expected to return at any moment from Silesia to defend Saxony.

10. 12-13 November: Gallas receives orders from Wallenstein to march with his 6,600 men from Bohemia into Saxony, to secure the region between Grimma and the Elbe.
11. Oberst Mohr vom Wald in the Meissen region (in the cities of Chemnitz, Nössen and Meissen, with HQ in Freiberg) is charged with keeping open communications with Gallas in Bohemia.
12. Two substantial 2500-3500 man detachments head for Altenburg and Zwickau. Most obey the recall order and return for the Lützen battle, except De Suys infantry regiment which continues to Zwickau, and Contreras' infantry regiment at Altenburg.
13. 15 November, c. 4.30am: Gustav Adolf marches out of the Naumburg camp, aiming to catch Wallenstein by surprise before he can reconcentrate his forces.
14. 15 November, 12-3pm: Skirmish at the Rippach stream, near the villages of Rippach (Hilpritz) and Poserna.

to garrison Grimma, and to prevent Saxon encroachments from the east. With Gallas in place the conquest of Saxony could continue as planned.

The dispersal of Wallenstein's army began on the morning of Sunday 14 November. Several regiments of Croats were left behind as a screen. Aside from Pappenheim's corps, which set off for Halle via Merseburg, the bulk of the army was to move with the generalissimo to Leipzig. Oberst Melchior von Hatzfeld, brother of the dispossessed bishop of Würzburg, was sent to Eilenburg with 3,000 men to hold off Saxon approaches from Torgau. Smaller detachments departed for other outlying towns. The pattern of troop dispersal more resembled a spider's web for detecting enemy activity than a quartering list for winter.

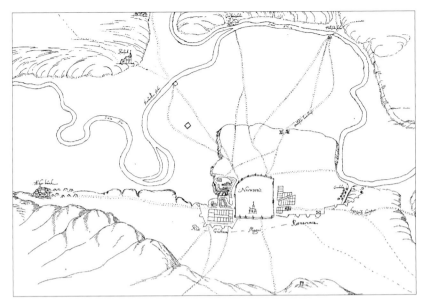

Matthias Gallas (1584–1647). Recently appointed Feldmarschall, he commanded a corps stationed on the Bohemian border with Saxony. A genial enough person, he was tactically incompetent, but because of the Imperialists' constant shortage of talented officers, was destined to succeed Wallenstein as commander-in-chief of the Emperor's forces. (From *Theatrum Europaeum*)

Gustav Adolf makes his move

On Sunday 14 November, scouts informed Gustav Adolf that Wallenstein was retreating from Weissenfels, and that Pappenheim's corps had split off, though it was unclear where they were heading. It was the opportunity the King had been waiting for. He proposed to his general staff an immediate strike while the enemy was divided. Bernhard was in favour, Knyphausen was more cautious and questioned the need for risking an open battle, but the King's mind was already made up.

Shortly after 4.00am (three hours before dawn) on Monday 15 November, the royal army began to leave the Naumburg camp, marching in battle order. Most of the baggage train was left in camp, and only 100 wagons carrying essential supplies accompanied the army as it slinked into the wintry morning gloom.

Initially, the march was directed towards the town of Pegau in the hope of linking up with Duke Georg of Lüneburg's 2,000 horse expected imminently from Torgau. But unwelcome news soon arrived: the Saxon commander-in-chief, Arnim, following his own agenda as usual, had forbidden Duke Georg from attempting to join the Swedes, fearing that it would compromise his own army in Silesia. Gustav Adolf huffed that the German princes refused to listen to his orders. Later in the morning, locals and farmers were able to give clearer news of Pappenheim's movements and the shift of Wallenstein's HQ. Gustav Adolf modified his march route accordingly, across the open country and minor roads south of Weissenfels, towards Lützen.

THE RIPPACH SKIRMISH, 15 NOVEMBER

On the morning of 15 November all was quiet in the Imperial rear at Weissenfels. The Imperial garrison of 100 men under Captain Delabonde[2] was inadequate to defend the town and was preparing to leave. Wallenstein's infantry commander, Generalwachtmeister Rudolf Colloredo, had arrived with a few companies of Croats, to escort Delabonde to safety. It was a fairly

Rudolf Freiherr von Colloredo (1585–1657). Although of Mediterranean origin he was born in Budweis, Bohemia, and spent most of his career north of the Alps. Trained in Tilly's army, he was promoted to Generalwachtmeister in 1632, giving him overall command of Wallenstein's infantry. Plodding rather than talented, his stand at the Rippach won Wallenstein the precious hours needed to reassemble much of his dispersed army.

routine morning, until Colloredo caught sight of the Swedish juggernaut advancing south of the town towards Leipzig. Despatching some Croats to warn Wallenstein, Colloredo beat a hasty retreat back towards Lützen along with Delabonde's men.

The Swedish advance guard, spotting Colloredo's force retiring parallel to their advance, gave chase. Uncharacteristically, the Croats stood and fought, losing a standard and a few dozen men while buying time for Colloredo to reach the defensible crossing points of a small river, the Rippach – a boggy tributary of the Saale. Gustav Adolf pushed on, but his advance came to an abrupt halt shortly after midday, 7km short of Lützen, at the 'filthy pass' (as Watts called it) across the Rippach. The Swedish plan 'to catch Wallenstein a sleeper' was about to be thwarted.

More by chance than foresight, Colloredo had several regiments at his disposal – in all about 500 dragoons and horse, most of them Croats. The Colonel-General of the Croats, Count Isolano, should have been well on his way to Merseburg according to Holk's orders, but 'because of his lust for Venus rather than Mars' (as the local chronicles describe it) had been delayed by amorous adventures at an inn, the *Gasthof zum Rippach.*

The main road to Leipzig crossed the Rippach at a bridge near the Rippach inn. There were also several lesser crossing points not designed for heavy traffic: the Poserna bridge, the first reached by the Swedish advance guard, could be crossed only 'one or two men abreast'. The Swedes made no attempt to rush the Rippach bridges. With Croats on the Wein-Berg heights (so-called after vineyards on the south-facing slopes) the crossings appeared well defended. The woods along the valley made Colloredo's strength difficult to estimate, so little was done until the main body of the 18,000-strong Swedish Army, began to arrive. The Swedes drew up in the same battle order they were to employ at Lützen: the right wing led by Gustav Adolf himself, the left by Bernhard and the centre by Knyphausen.

According to local chronicles, the Swedes were unable to cross the stream until a local shepherd, Assmussen, showed them a ford near the Feld Mühle watermill, about 1.5km west of Rippach village. At about

RIGHT **At the time of the battle the Rippach stream was about 7–8 metres broad and 1–2 metres deep, with a muddy bottom. As much of an obstacle were the swampy banks, swollen by late autumn rain, which extended into water meadows as much as 200 metres broad. The modern Rippach bridge is seen here from the east, with Rippach village on the right.**

THE SKIRMISH AT THE RIPPACH

1. c.12.00pm: Retiring from Weissenfels, Colloredo with a few companies of Croats and the former Weissenfels garrison crosses the Rippach stream to safety. The Swedish advance guard does not attempt to follow. Colloredo improvises a defence line on the heights north of the Rippach stream.
2. c.1.00pm: The former garrison of Weissenfels under Captain Delabonde continue their retreat towards Lützen to avoid capture.
3. c.1.00–2.00pm: Main elements of the Swedish army marching from Naumburg along minor roads and cross-country begin to arrive and are put into battle order.
4. 2.00pm: Guided by a local shepherd, Protestant cavalry (presumably of Bernhard's wing) cross a ford near the Feld Mühle watermill, and break

Imperial cavalry sent to intercept them.
5. c.2.15–2.45pm: The 3-pdr regimental cannon attached to the commanded musketeers of the Swedish right wing under Count von Eberstein fire on Croat formations on the heights west of Poserna village, forcing them to fall back. A bridgehead over the Rippach is established.
6. c.3.00–3.30pm: With the Rippach village and bridge outflanked, Colloredo's troops fall back towards Lützen without further significant loss.
7. 3.00pm–4.30pm: After crossing the various Rippach bridges and fords, the King's Army reaches the plain, and makes headway towards Lützen, 6–7km distant. With darkness falling Gustav Adolf takes the decision to camp rather than to engage Wallenstein that evening.

2.00pm Protestant cavalry squadrons crossed the ford, and defeated an Imperial horse unit, whose standard they captured, establishing a foothold on the north bank.

Shortly afterwards the Swedish right wing moved to cross at Poserna three kilometres away. Opposing the Swedes were Croats lining the hills (one of them now named the 'Kroaten-Berg') on the far bank. Accompanying the Scandinavian horsemen were five 200-man bodies of 'commanded musketeers' (detached from their regiments), each with two regimental guns, under the overall command of Oberst Eberstein. From these cannon Count Eberstein fired a few volleys at the Croats, who fell back from the heights, giving Eberstein's musketeers room to establish a bridgehead. The Swedish horse quickly followed.

With the crossing at Poserna secure, the skirmish was quickly over. By 3.00pm Gustav Adolf's troops were filing across the Rippach, and by 4.00pm they were tramping over open country towards Lützen. But on

ABOVE **Johann Ludwig Graf Isolano (1586–1640).** A Cypriot noble greatly trusted by Wallenstein, in January 1632 he became '*Oberst-Kommandant* of all Croats and light horse in Imperial service'. English prisoners captured by his Croats described him as 'an old beardless man, full of the palsie and a Gentleman of much valour, courtesie and extraordinary hardinesse of body'. (*Theatrum Europaeum*, Vol. IV, 1st edn)

RIGHT **Wallenstein's order to Pappenheim (soaked in Pappenheim's blood) ordering him to hurry back to Lützen:** 'The enemy is marching towards us. Your honour shall drop everything, and route himself hereto with all troops and guns, to be with us in the early morning.' There is an interesting postscript referring to the boggy Rippach crossing: '[The enemy] is already at the pass where yesterday the road was bad.' (Heeres Museum, Vienna)

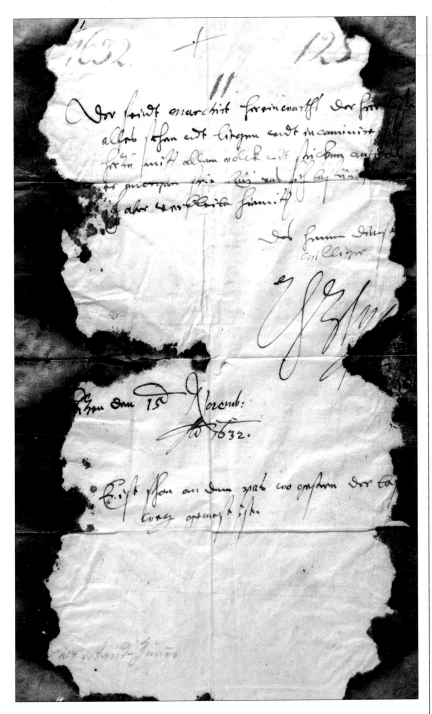

this cold November day, the sun set soon after 4.00pm and darkness and mist were already falling. 'If only we had three more hours of daylight' Gustav Adolf lamented to his officers. Reluctantly he decided to make camp; the battle would have to wait until morning. Morale remained high in the Protestant ranks. Upwards of 50 of the enemy had been killed and two standards taken, for little loss.

Colloredo's warning of the approach of the Swedish Army reached Wallenstein in the early afternoon, just as the Rippach action was beginning. Wallenstein had to think quickly – to stand or retreat on Leipzig? His decision (not taken lightly since he disliked fighting in the open) was, as Holk later wrote, 'not to retreat one foot'. Only Wallenstein had the authority to reassemble the army and it appears that it was him not Colloredo who gave the pre-arranged signal of three cannon-shots to bring in the outlying detachments.[3] Wallenstein then penned the famous letter to Pappenheim, ordering him to return immediately to Lützen. The Rippach skirmish had won Wallenstein a night's grace to regroup his army. Holk later wrote that without that breathing space, the Swedish King would have 'achieved a great effect' on Wallenstein's unprepared force.

As darkness fell, the Imperial watch-fires could be seen from the Swedish lines. The armies were separated by a distance that Holk estimated as no more than four cannon shots and Colonel Fleetwood with the Swedes, at 'about an English myle'. The Imperial troops got little rest that night. Holk rearranged them by candle-light, slotting units into the battle line as they arrived in response to Wallenstein's signal. Meanwhile the Swedes, having advanced without tents, slept in the open, 'every Regiment lying downe, in the same order that they marched, with their armes by them'. Gustav Adolf retired to his carriage, while his senior commanders, including both dukes of Weimar, bedded down nearby 'having nothing over their heads, but the Heavenly Arch, nor any thing under them, but trusses of straw layd upon the Earth'.

It was about midnight when Pappenheim received Wallenstein's order to march. His troops were dispersed in and around Halle, after a day's hard plundering, and it was 2.00am before he was able to leave, accompanied by his cavalry and dragoons. Moving the artillery in the dark was considered impractical, and so they were left with the infantry, under Pappenheim's second-in-command, Generalwachtmeister Reinach, with instructions to move at first light.

---

1   According to local tradition the Imperial staff conference in Weissenfels took place on 12 November.
2   Holk's dispersal plan for 14 November provided for 300 men from Comargo's and Reinach's infantry regiments to garrison Weissenfels. It is not clear if these were the same as the force commanded by Delabonde.
3   Berlepsch notes that the signal originated from the Imperial Headquarters.

THE BATTLE,
16 NOVEMBER

The Imperial deployments

Wallenstein had decided to make his stand at the small town of Lützen, about 14km north-east of Weissenfels and 20km south-west of Leipzig. Built around a toll station on the Frankfurt–Leipzig *Landstrasse*, it was a location that often witnessed the passage of armies, travelling from the German heartlands to the north-east.

Lützen contained a small, moated stone castle at its south-west corner and about 300 primitively built houses, enclosed by a town wall. The town stood in a region of pancake-flat farmland. To the west this was boggy meadow, to the east it was somewhat firmer, being drained by two canals. The first of these waterways, a mill race called the Mühlgraben, was easily jumped; the Flossgraben was more substantial and could only be crossed by bridge.

Wallenstein based his position on the Leipzig post road, one of the best in Germany. The road went out north-east from Lützen for about 2.5km before crossing the Flossgraben. Either side of the road were drainage ditches (then dry), which Wallenstein dug out to create two long and deep trenches. Close to the town, north of the road were three windmills standing on a very shallow hill. It was here that Wallenstein constructed an emplacement for his artillery. A ring of gardens surrounded Lützen. These had man-high mud walls, which could be easily loopholed – ideal shelter for musketeers. It was in these gardens that some of the hottest fighting of the day would occur.

Wallenstein had drawn up his battle line in a manner ideally suited for defence: it was deep, compact and allowed for transfer of units between wings. The Imperial infantry was ordered in three lines, with five bodies in the first, two in the second and one in reserve. Holk, who was personally responsible for putting the troops into formation, gives further details in his account of the battle, stating that the front line was of '5000 on foot in five brigades; the middle of two brigades each of 1000 and six companies of horse intermixed 2 by 2; and last stood outcommanded five companies of 500 men on foot, and two squadrons of 12 companies of horse.' Holk's wording makes it clear that the third 'line' consisted of a single 500-man body of five companies, and that these were 'outcommanded' – that is, musketeers serving without pikemen.

The Imperial cavalry was deployed mostly on the wings, echeloned back to prevent outflanking. The Croats were mainly on Wallenstein's left wing, acting as a screen for the army ('the crabates haveing the lefte wynge', according to Fleetwood), but there was also a detachment on the right, as shown on the Weissenfels plan and Snayers' painting. According to Holk: 'On each wing 150 musketeers stood in front of the Horse.' These were probably not deployed in Swedish style, 'interlined' among the cavalry, more likely they huddled in the roadside ditches.

CROATS AT THE RIPPACH
The skirmish at the Rippach stream delayed Gustav Adolf's army by several hours and lost him the element of surprise. At the beginning of the action the Swedish advance guard (probably Finns) caught up with a few companies of Croat horsemen and took one of their standards. The flag, painted on one side with the Imperial eagle and on the other with 'Fortune' (personified on a cannon ball), was seen as an omen that the next day would go well. 'But the King tooke no great content at it,' wrote Watts, 'being sorry ... that night had prevented him from taking more of them.' (Graham Turner)

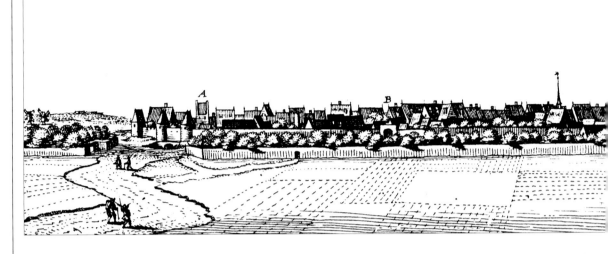

The imperial cannon were deployed in two main batteries, anchoring the infantry line at both ends, and positioned so that their fire would sweep through troops advancing on the Imperial centre. The 'windmill battery' was the larger, numbering 14–17 cannon, including five 24-pdrs, four 12-pdrs and four 6-pdrs. The left-wing battery, posted among the ditches on the far left of the line, numbered six or seven guns, including four 24-pdrs and two 12-pdrs. Protestant sources indicate two further batteries in the middle of the Imperial line; these were probably regimental cannon attached to the infantry brigades.

The 1,000-man infantry 'brigades' mentioned by Holk were, in effect, battalion formations – proof that Wallenstein was well aware of the manoeuvrability of smaller formations and had abandoned the *tercio*. The Imperial cavalry were fielded in 'squadrons', which were essentially regiment sized. The cuirassiers were all deployed in the front part of the line, where they could give direct support to the infantry, or in a double squadron on each wing, able to deliver a decisive punch. The harquebusier regiments, many of which had been raised as little as three months earlier, were deployed further back on the wings and in the third line: Wallenstein clearly realised they would be of limited value.

With Pappenheim absent, command of the battle line had an improvised nature. The energetic Holk took the left wing, but would hand over to Pappenheim on his arrival. Generalwachtmeister Rudolf Colloredo commanded the infantry centre assisted by two infantry brigade commanders: Oberst Berthold von Waldstein, known as 'Young Wallenstein', a relative of the generalissimo, who conducted the right of the line, and Oberst Francesco Grana Marchese di Caretto, who led the left. Of the three infantry commanders only 'Young Wallenstein' had any special military talent. Grana not only lacked ability, but was unpopular to boot, and owed his position to his smarmy court manners (eventually intriguing his way to a field marshal's baton). He was, none the less, at the head of his regiment in the heat of the battle when it mattered most.

Wallenstein took charge of the right wing, but did not remain there all the battle. Far from being confined by gout to his sedan chair (as the French pamphlet, *Le Soldat Suedois*, claims he was) he spent the battle on horseback: 'His Excellency shewed that day no ordinary valour, riding up

LEFT **The Flossgraben (literally 'float-dyke') was named after the floating wood it carried. It was dug in the 1580s to transport firewood for two nearby salt refineries and originally had a 'U' cross-section and was several metres broad and deep. It flowed round the south and east of the battlefield and was a considerable obstacle to troop movement.**

and downe the Front of all the Regiments; where from time to time necessity call'd him: encouraging with his presence, everybody to the accomplishment of their duty.' (*Spanish Relation*, p.162)

The Swedes approach, 7.30–9.00am

A dense fog had come down in the night: 'A gentle mist, as if foredooming how black a day it would be.' For the Swedes this fog made another pre-dawn start impractical, and the reveille seems to have been sounded only shortly before first light (about 7.30am) on Tuesday morning, 16 November (6 November old style).[4]

The King's army would have been ready to march in minutes: it had camped in battle order and there were no tents to pack, but it was impossible to make headway in the fog. The gloomy time was filled by morning service, the King's prayers directed by the army chaplain Dr Fabricius. Afterwards, Gustav Adolf gave two rousing speeches to encourage his troops.

BATTLE OF LÜTZEN, INITIAL DISPOSITIONS AT 11.00AM, 16 NOVEMBER 1632

To Halle

To Leipzig

'Fake' troops

Loyers & Lohe

Imperial Baggage

Leutersheim

Goschütz

Piccolomini

Isolano Croats

Tontinelli (=Lindelo)

Westrumb

"commanded companies"

Götz

Baden

Westfalen

GFZM Breuner

Comargo

Drost

Jung-Breuner

Breda

F. Breuner & Grana

Finland horse

Hagen

Colloredo & Chiesa

Västgöta horse

Trčka & Desfours

B. Wallenstein & Alt-Sachsen

Södermanland horse

Duke Wilhelm's

Holk

Uppland horse

Goldstein

Musketeers

Ostgöta horse

Bulach

Windmills

Småland horse

Beckermann

Miller's House

Swedish Brigade

Hessians

Croats

Yellow (Guards) Brigade

Georg v. Uslar

LÜTZEN

1st line reserve (Henderson's musketeers)

Duke Wilhelm's Brigade

Old Blue Brigade

Knyphausen's (White) Brigade

Lützen Castle

Bernhard's (Green) Brigade

2nd line reserve (Öhm)

Bernhard's Leibregiment

Thurn's Brigade

Swedish Baggage

Bernhard's Leibregiment

Mitzlaff's Brigade

Carberg

Hofkirch (Saxons)

Kurland horse

Livonian horse

Ernst of Anhalt (Saxons)

Swedish Baggage

Courville

Löwenstein

To Weissenfels & Naumburg

Brandenstein

Steinbach

Stechenitz

Meuchen (Chursitz)

Eberstein, commanded musketeers among cavalry

Gersdorf, commanded musketeers among cavalry

Muhlgraben

Gardens

Mud Wall

Flossgraben

N

| 0 | 500 yds |
| 0 | 500 m |

44

The Lützen windmills were the site of the main Imperial artillery battery and saw some of the day's heaviest fighting. Damaged during the battle (one source states that Wallenstein dismantled them to create a firing position for his artillery), they were later rebuilt in much the same form, as seen here shortly before 1902/03, when they were finally demolished. The shallow hill on which they stood is no longer visible today and could have stood no more than a metre or two above the plain. (Museum im Schloss Lützen)

First he addressed his Swedes and Finns: *'You true valiant brethren! See that you doe valiantly carry yourselves this day, fighting bravely for God's Word and your King; which if you doe, so will you have mercy of God and honour before the world; and I will truely reward you; but if you doe not, I sweare unto you that your bones shall never come in Sweden againe.'*

Next he harangued the German troops: *'You true and worthy* Deutsch *brethren, Officers and common soldiers! I exhort you all, carry yourselves manfully and fight truely with me. Runne not away and I shall hazard my body and bloud with you for your best. If you stand with me, so I hope in God to obtaine victory, the profit whereof will redownd to you and your successors. And if otherwise you doe, so are you and your liberties lost.'*[5]

With the morning mist beginning to lift, Gustav Adolf called his men to advance. Then, gazing to the heavens, he called in the top of his voice: 'Jesus, Jesus, Jesus! Help me this day to fight for the glory of thy holy name!' The march began.

Meanwhile the Imperial army was also stirring. Those soldiers who could be spared from entrenchment work heard mass and confessed their sins. But it was not Wallenstein's custom to give pep-talks: he remained silent, 'his stern countenance being enough to remind his men of the punishments they might endure or the rich rewards awaiting them if they served well' (Richelieu's memoirs).

Despite the fog, the King's army was on the march soon after 8.00am. The army had camped about halfway between Lützen and Rippach, and it would have taken no more than an hour to reach Lützen, although Croat horsemen from the Imperial Army did their best to impede the advance. The first sightings of Swedish troops from the main Imperial lines occurred at 8.30am, according to Catholic broadsheets, while the Swedish Army caught its first sight of the Imperial battle order at about 9.00am (Dalbier).

The most widely copied plans of the battle were published in 1633 at Frankfurt am Main by the Dutch engraver Friedrich van Hulsen (Hulsius) in an appendix to the geographical work *Inventarium Sueciae*. (Inventory of Sweden). He had accurate information about the Swedish order of battle supplied by participants, but reconstructed Wallenstein's deployments from earlier prints. Wallenstein's infantry is shown drawn up (incorrectly) in Spanish *tercios* (four in the centre and one on the right).

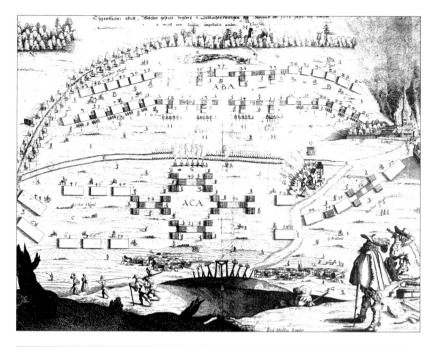

A rare coloured plan of the battle, in gouache on parchment, either based on van Hulsen's plan or the source for it. The two foreground figures are engineer-cartographers, giving the false impression that the picture was drawn from life. They appear reversed right to left on several prints of the battle. (Germanisches Nationalmuseum, Nuremberg)

OPPOSITE, BELOW The Imperial deployments from Bianchi's portrait, no doubt based on information from one of Wallenstein's Italian officers. The infantry (marked A) is shown correctly with five blocks in the front line and one (instead of two) in the second. The cavalry (D) is echeloned back on both wings, with further detachments behind the infantry. Piccolomini's regiment (G) is the second squadron on the left flank. Gustav Adolf's death site is at 'H' on the Imperial left, not far from Pappenheim's at 'F'. The modern view that Pappenheim detoured through Leipzig is contradicted by 'E', which states that he arrived 'pere il Camine d'Alla' – by the road from Halle.

From a vantage point on the Weissenfels road the Saxon liaison officer, Berlepsch, saw four bodies of horse beside the town of Lützen standing 'completely still'– probably Croat horsemen posted ahead of the main Imperial line. Beyond them was 'a front of Horse and Foot near the windmills at the town'. Berlepsch added that 'The marching music of more men moving forward could be clearly made out'.

The meadows to the west of Lützen were too waterlogged to support troops, let alone cannon. Instead, Gustav Adolf made for the open plain to the east, keen to engage the main Imperial position. There were still to be two hours of frustrating delay, not caused by fog, but by the Flossgraben and Muhlgraben streams, which blocked access to the chosen battlefield. All 18,000 Swedish troops did not, of course, cross the bridge at the village of Meuchen (on some maps called Chursitz). Nor did they wade the icy waters of the Flossgraben: on such a cold day no general would order his men to cross if he valued their health and respect. Using the plentiful supply of wood floating on the Flossgraben, the Swedes improvised makeshift bridges across the waterway. Even so, the ammunition wagons and big guns had to detour several kilometres over the Meuchen bridge, and Gustav Adolf reluctantly decided to start the battle before they were all in position.

The Swedish battle array

The Swedish army's battle order was not decided upon suddenly on the foggy morning of 16 November. Shuffling 18,000 men into formation, without rehearsal and under fire, would only have resulted in chaos. The battle order had already been determined at Naumburg, along with the allocation of regiments to brigades and squadrons, so that when the army marched out of camp on the 15th, it was already in the formation it would adopt at Lützen. A 90-degree turn of the component brigades and squadrons would transform the marching formation into a battle order.

The battle order was made up of two 'fronts' or lines, with intervals between units. These gaps allowed first line units that became disordered to retire behind the second line, where they could safely re-form. In action the intervals were occupied by the artillery attached to the brigades.

Gustav Adolf took the traditional position of honour on the right wing. Duke Bernhard was second in command and took the left wing, while Knyphausen was third in command, and took charge of the reserve. There was a degree of redundancy of commands, so that control could be maintained if commanders were disabled. GenMaj Nils Brahe was commander of the front line of four infantry brigades, yet the King also exerted control over the right-most of these, the Swedish and Yellow brigades. Duke Bernhard, meanwhile, had jurisdiction over the left-most infantry brigades. Knyphausen directly commanded the rear four

Equestrian portrait of Gustav Adolf, by Giovanni Paolo Bianchi of Milan. Below the Swedish King is an unusually accurate (and previously unpublished) plan of the Imperial deployments at Lützen. (Anne S.K. Brown Military Collection)

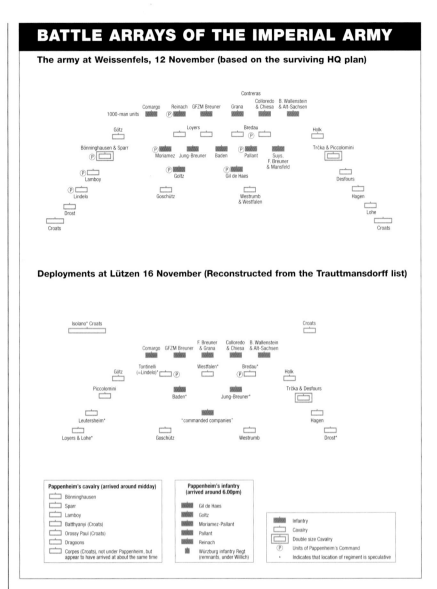

BATTLE ARRAYS OF THE IMPERIAL ARMY

The army at Weissenfels, 12 November (based on the surviving HQ plan)

Contreras

Comargo · Reinach · GFZM Breuner · Grana · Colloredo & Chiesa · B. Wallenstein & Alt-Sachsen

1000-man units

Götz · Loyers · Bredau · Holk

Bönninghausen & Sparr · Moriamez · Jung-Breuner · Baden · Pallant · Suys, F. Breuner & Mansfeld · Trčka & Piccolomini

Lamboy · Goltz · Gil de Haes · Desfours

Lindelo · Goschütz · Westrumb & Westfalen · Hagen

Drost · Lohe

Croats · Croats

Deployments at Lützen 16 November (Reconstructed from the Trauttmansdorff list)

Isolano* Croats · Croats

Comargo · GFZM Breuner · F. Breuner & Grana · Colloredo & Chiesa · B. Wallenstein & Alt-Sachsen

Götz · Tontinelli (=Lindelo)* · Westfalen* · Bredau* · Holk

Piccolomini · Baden* · Jung-Breuner* · Trčka & Desfours

Leutersheim* · "commanded companies" · Hagen

Loyers & Lohe* · Goschütz · Westrumb · Drost*

Pappenheim's cavalry (arrived around midday)
- Bönninghausen
- Sparr
- Lamboy
- Batthyanyi (Croats)
- Orossy Paul (Croats)
- Dragoons
- Corpes (Croats), not under Pappenheim, but appear to have arrived at about the same time

Pappenheim's infantry (arrived around 6.00pm)
- Gil de Haes
- Goltz
- Moriamez-Pallant
- Pallant
- Reinach
- Würzburg infantry Regt (remnants, under Willich)

Key:
- Infantry
- Cavalry
- Double size Cavalry
- (P) Units of Pappenheim's Command
- * Indicates that location of regiment is speculative

The battle order of the Imperial army has long been one of the battle's most perplexing issues. The recent discovery by Stadler of the Trauttmansdorff list in the Austrian state archives has greatly simplified the problem of identifying the unit positions. The 5:2:1 arrangement of infantry brigades was a modification of the 6:5:2 formation employed four days earlier at Weissenfels, and was the simplest way of coping with the army's reduced size. When Pappenheim's troops arrived they were to be tacked on at the rear.

Trauttmansdorff's list of Imperial regiments that fought at Lützen

[Infantry]
- A Pertoldt von Walstein and Alt-Sachsen
- B Coloredo and Chiesa [i.e. Kehraus]
- C Grana and Fridrich Breiner
- D Alt-Preuner [i.e. Feldzeugmeister Breuner]
- E Camargo
- F Baden
- G Jung-Breiner [i.e. Hans Gottfried Breuner]
- H Commanded companies

[Cavalry]
- J Holckhe
- K Terzka and des Four
- L Haagen
- M Droost
- N Breda
- O Westpfalen
- P Tontinelli
- Q Isolani
- R Göz
- S Piccolomini
- T Leudersshaimb
- V Loyers and Lohe
- Y Westromb
- X Gouchier [Goschütz]

[Pappenheim's Horse]
- & Corpes [Croats]
- + Bonigkhausen
- ▶ Sparr
- O Lamboi
- ★ Batthiani [Croats]
- 4 Orossi Paul [Croats]
- zz Dragoons

Source: Österreichisches Staatsarchiv, Vienna; Familienarchiv Trauttmansdorff, manuscript 98 f.112. The list was first published by Stadler p.891 (see Further Reading) but with Piccolomini's Regiment accidentally omitted. The letters and non-alphabetical symbols are keys to a missing battle plan.

---

infantry brigades, but in practice was also responsible for the entire reserve line of cavalry. When Gustav Adolf or Bernhard needed fresh cavalry squadrons, they requested these from Knyphausen.

Stålhandske had command of the front line of the right-wing cavalry, Bulach of the rear-right. The front-left was directly under Duke Bernhard in his capacity as Generalmajor of cavalry. The rear-left was probably commanded by Bernhard's elder brother, Duke Ernst of Weimar.

The infantry were drawn up in 'Swedish brigades' – temporary formations, built up from several regiments. In theory these were drawn up six deep, in practice in weaker brigades, as little as four deep. The Yellow and (Old) Blue brigades were composed of a single large regiment, of the same name. Confusingly the Swedish brigade was also sometimes known as the Blue Brigade, after its main component unit, the 'New Blue' Regiment. Duke Bernhard's (Green) Brigade had nothing in common with the Green Brigade that fought at Breitenfeld under Sir John Hepburn, but was named after an entirely different unit,

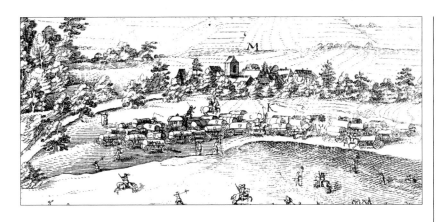

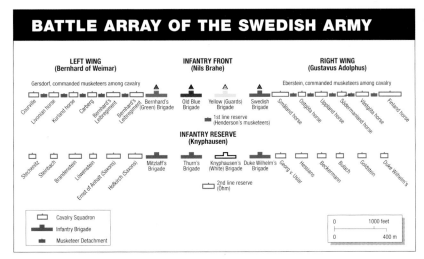

BATTLE ARRAY OF THE SWEDISH ARMY

Duke Bernhard's (Green) Leibregiment. It is coincidence that the Scots of the army happened to be concentrated in this brigade under Oberstleutnant Ludovick Leslie.

The tactical formation of the Swedish horse was the squadron, in theory, four companies strong. Because of campaign losses, especially in horses, few regiments were able to field more than a single squadron, only Duke Bernhard's and Stålhandske's deployed in two, while the Hessian cavalry were so weak that no less than four regiments made up one squadron. Squadrons varied from 80 to 400 men and were deployed three or four deep.

THE FIRST SWEDISH ATTACKS, 10.00AM–12.00PM

With the sun climbing, Gustav Adolf waited impatiently as his troops crossed the Flossgraben. Wallenstein made little response: a few musket shots whistled out from Lützen town when any Swedes came close, but the Imperial artillery remained silent.

At about 10.00am the King ordered a small battery of (three to five) demi-cannon to open fire. Wallenstein was in no hurry to reply with his

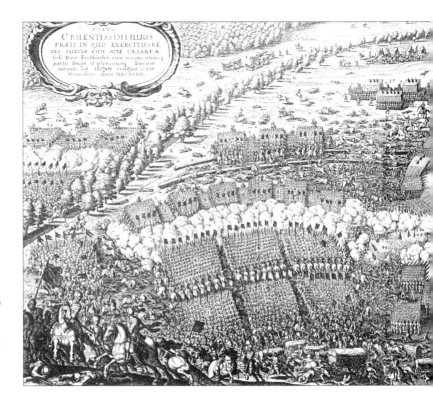

BELOW **The battle order published in *The Swedish Intelligencer*, Part 3, in 1633, showed the Imperial army as it appeared to the Swedes – a single line. In addition to the two main Imperial batteries, the illustrator showed pairs of cannon (regimental guns?) in the middle of the line. Note also the concentration of baggage-wagons on the Imperial left.**

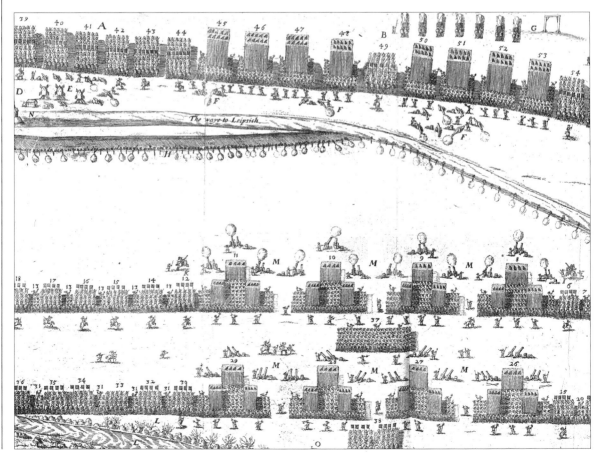

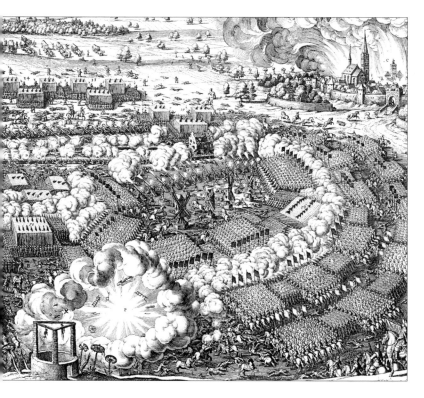

far larger batteries, awaiting a better target. When they eventually opened up, one of the first Swedish casualties (according to a perhaps apocryphal account) was the piebald horse with 'pretty ears' of a young French captain, Jean de Hontas de Gassion (a later marshal of France), killed with the first round. Gustav Adolf had problems with his own horse which, alarmed by the cannon fire, refused to move. 'This does not bode well for me; the battle may be rather difficult,' the King was heard to say, before switching to a calmer steed. The artillery exchange continued for about an hour, without serious losses on either side.

Fearing outflanking, Gustav Adolf requested Knyphausen to release three squadrons from his second line, to 'imp out the feathers' of his right wing. These squadrons, Bulach's, Goldstein's and Duke Wilhelm's, duly marched to the far right to cover any Croat threat.

The total Protestant strength at this point was slightly more than 18,000 men. Facing them was Wallenstein's force rumoured to be 30,000 strong, but in reality little more than 12,000. Further small detachments continued to arrive during the day. Elements of Pappenheim's force including Bredau's and Tontinelli's cavalry, which had presumably not reached Halle the day before, were able to take up their positions before the battle got underway.

It was at this point that Wallenstein had Lützen set on fire. The town walls were in poor repair and Holk estimated that 1,000 soldiers were needed to defend the place: he could spare only 400. Rather than risk losing the town and being outflanked, Wallenstein preferred to deny it to both sides. With typical thoroughness, he first rounded up the townsfolk and locked them in the castle cellars to prevent them from putting out the fires. Holk's 400 musketeers took their posts in the castle and behind the mud-walls of the gardens ringing the town.

51

A transcript of the only surviving sketch of the battle, made by a member of the Swedish Army whose post was probably among the second line cavalry of the Swedish left. His scribbled annotations show that the line's deployment differed slightly from the published Swedish plans, with from left to right: Brandenstein, Hertzog Ernst [of Weimar]. 3 cornets [Stechenitz?], Steinbach, [Prince Ernst of] Anhalt, and Hofkirch. He notes that the Swedish horse stood 3 deep, while the Imperialists were 6 deep. At the bottom are criss-cross patterns captioned 'Das Flosholtz ober dem graben' (Float-wood over the dyke) – evidence that the Swedes crossed the Flossgraben on makeshift bridges constructed from floating wood. The original ink sketch is in the Stockholm Krigsarkivet.

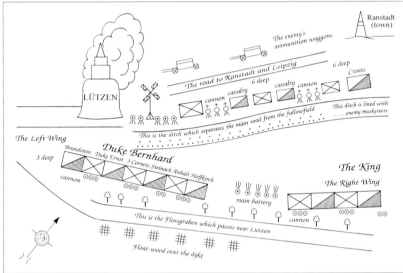

A gentle breeze fanned the flames in Lützen, and blew straight onto the advancing Swedes and, as Fleetwood noted, caused them 'much inconvenience, the wind bloweing the smoak just upon us'. According to the Swedish field-chancellery diary it was 'such a thick fog that one could barely see another at four paces'. It was the smoke from Lützen, rather than the morning mist, which was to cause such confusion in the early stages of the battle.

With the royal army over the Flossgraben and back in two neat battle lines, the advance could at last begin. At about 11.00am Gustav Adolf had his field trumpeter, Jöns Månsson Thet, play Psalm 46 – *Eine feste Burg ist unser Gott*. Followed by Psalm 67: *Es wolt uns Gott genädig sein*, which the King himself sang 'very loudly'. It had become a Protestant army tradition to sing these psalms (noted Montecuccoli) and, before the second had finished, to begin the advance.

Imperial officers like Silvio Piccolomini, a *rittmeister* in his uncle Ottavio's regiment, watched in awe as the Swedish battle line began to trundle forward 'in the most beautiful order'. The line began as one coherent front, about 2.5km long, but as the action unfolded and the Lützen 'fog' came down ever thicker, sections of the line began to act

As the Swedish Army prepared its first assault, Wallenstein deliberately set light to Lützen. The castle (C) was the only major building to escape the conflagration. Detail of the Lützen battleplan from *Theatrum Europaeum*, vol II.

independently. The reserve line under Knyphausen kept 500–600 paces behind the first line – far enough to avoid artillery fire and local confusion.

Actions on the Swedish right

It was on the Swedish right wing where, in Holk's words, 'All the fury began'. On this wing, Gustav Adolf had at his disposal the six regiments of Swedish and Finnish horse, the cream of his cavalry. Between their squadrons, as at the Rippach, were five 200-man bodies of 'commanded musketeers' each with two attached regimental cannon. Also part of the actions on this wing were the two right-most brigades of the infantry centre under Count Nils Brahe.

Immediately to the front of the wing were several bodies of Croat horsemen – a screen to hide the weakness of the Imperial left. Unarmoured, on light horses and in loose formations, they posed little threat to the Swedes and Finns. Behind them, however, Gustav Adolf could make out several bodies of Imperial cuirassiers, with their ominous black armour and dark horses. He called to Torsten Stålhandske, the

In the opening attack Gustav Adolf sent his Finnish horse to chase off the Croat screen on the Imperial left. Recognisable by their colourful eastern clothing, the Croats fled back onto the Imperial baggage-train, looting it and spreading confusion. Detail from Jacques Courtois' *Battle of Lützen*, which was commissioned in the 1650s by a participant, the Emperor's nephew Mattias de' Medici. (Pitti, Florence)

In an attempt to disguise the weakness of his left wing Wallenstein put his camp followers, wagon drivers and baggage boys into ad hoc battle formations. He intended to dismiss them as soon as Pappenheim arrived, but due to the ferocity of Gustav Adolf's attack his plan backfired and the non-combatants fled for safety, spreading panic in the Imperial rear. (Detail from Snayers' *Battle of Lützen*)

colonel of his Finns: 'As for those fellowes (meaning the Crabats) I care not for them,' saies the King: 'but charge me those blacke fellowes soundly: for they are the men that will undoe us.' (Watts)

Stålhandske set to the task. Taking half the squadrons of the front line with him, he advanced, veering north-east to cross the Leipzig road where the ditches had not been dug out by Wallenstein's troops. The Croats fled without exchanging blows. The Imperial echelon formation allowed Stålhandske's advance to make rapid headway, so that before long he had pushed forward so far that (as Berlepsch commented) the riders had 'their backs almost turned toward Ranstadt' – a village halfway to Leipzig.

Wallenstein had organised a number of mock formations to bulk out his weak left wing. Made up of camp followers and baggage hands with sheets as flags, these fake troops were panicked by the scattering of the Croats and by Stålhandske's sudden appearance. The chaos was compounded by rumours that Wallenstein had ordered the baggage to evacuate to Leipzig. Soon Croats and baggage hands were looting their own baggage, and the whole screaming mass was flying from the battlefield.

Meanwhile Gustav Adolf advanced with the inner squadrons of the Swedish right wing. Already at some distance from the Leipzig road he came under accurate fire from musketeers in the roadside ditches. One shot struck the Småland colonel, Fredrik Stenbock, in the foot. Clearing the ditches was work for the commanded musketeers under Count Eberstein. Separating out from the intervals between the cavalry, they advanced with their regimental cannon and soon had the enemy musketeers running for safety. But the parallel ditches proved to be impassable to cavalry. Gustav Adolf had little option but to leave Eberstein's musketeers holding the ditches, while he moved east along the road to find a crossing point.

Further towards the centre of the Swedish line, initially in one continuous front with Gustav Adolf's cavalry, Brahe led forward two infantry brigades, the Swedish and the Yellow, his objective the small Imperial battery on the Imperial left flank. A gap had opened in the

On the Imperial right the gap between mills and town was filled by cavalry echeloned back. A body of Croats was deployed slightly forward of them as can be seen in this detail from Snayers' *Battle of Lützen* painting. (Kunsthistorisches Museum, Vienna)

centre of the battlefield, separating these two brigades from Winckel's Blue Brigade, which was initially tasked to assist Bernhard on the left. [6]

The Imperialists watched Brahe's infantry advancing 'with notable resolution'. Cannon balls from the seven-gun ditch battery tore holes in the Swedish brigade, sweeping away entire ranks, but were unable to stop its measured advance 'our artillery being never able to disorder it though many a shot was made upon it' wrote the author of the *Spanish Relation*. The few hundred Imperial musketeers in the ditches were speedily ejected and replaced by Swedish musketeers, while the Swedish brigade overran the ditch battery and spiked the guns. The first objective in the centre had been taken.

All in all, the advance on the right wing had gone well. Stålhandske was now well over the Leipzig road, threatening to outflank the Imperialists. Gustav Adolf had cleared the ditch to his front, while Count Brahe had possession of the Imperial ditch battery.

The Swedish left: Bernhard's first assault

On the Swedish left wing Bernhard was confronted with a more difficult task than the King. In front of him was Wallenstein's powerful 'windmill' battery and the miller's house, fortified and full of Imperial musketeers; to his left was Lützen in flames, the gardens surrounding the town riddled with enemy musketeers who had loopholed the mud-brick walls. As on the King's wing everything was screened by Croat horsemen. It might have been enough for Bernhard to pin the Imperialists at this position and allow Gustav Adolf to lap round on his wing, but it was crucial to overwhelm Wallenstein before Pappenheim could return.

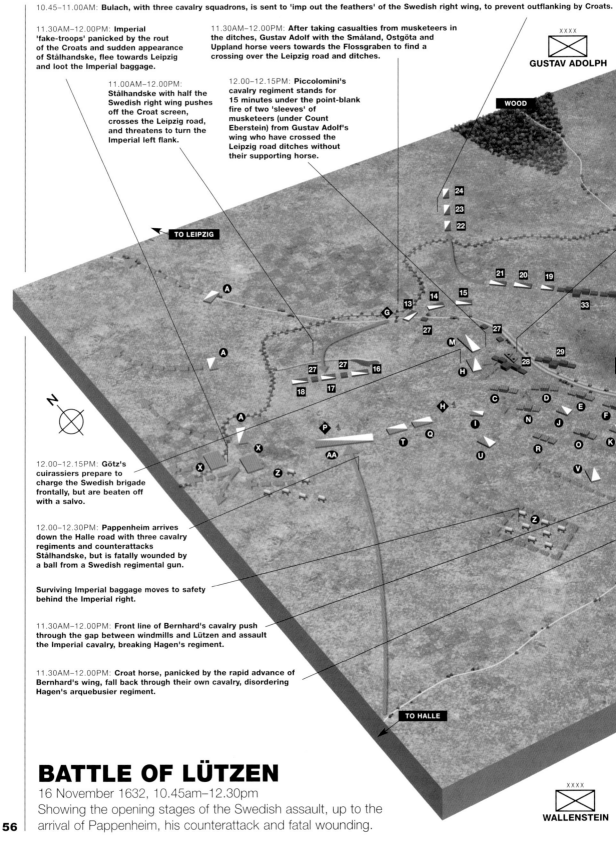

10.45–11.00AM: Bulach, with three cavalry squadrons, is sent to 'imp out the feathers' of the Swedish right wing, to prevent outflanking by Croats.

11.30AM–12.00PM: Imperial 'fake-troops' panicked by the rout of the Croats and sudden appearance of Stålhandske, flee towards Leipzig and loot the Imperial baggage.

11.30AM–12.00PM: After taking casualties from musketeers in the ditches, Gustav Adolf with the Småland, Ostgöta and Uppland horse veers towards the Flossgraben to find a crossing over the Leipzig road and ditches.

11.00AM–12.00PM: Stålhandske with half the Swedish right wing pushes off the Croat screen, crosses the Leipzig road, and threatens to turn the Imperial left flank.

12.00–12.15PM: Piccolomini's cavalry regiment stands for 15 minutes under the point-blank fire of two 'sleeves' of musketeers (under Count Eberstein) from Gustav Adolf's wing who have crossed the Leipzig road ditches without their supporting horse.

GUSTAV ADOLPH

WOOD

TO LEIPZIG

12.00–12.15PM: Götz's cuirassiers prepare to charge the Swedish brigade frontally, but are beaten off with a salvo.

12.00–12.30PM: Pappenheim arrives down the Halle road with three cavalry regiments and counterattacks Stålhandske, but is fatally wounded by a ball from a Swedish regimental gun.

Surviving Imperial baggage moves to safety behind the Imperial right.

11.30AM–12.00PM: Front line of Bernhard's cavalry push through the gap between windmills and Lützen and assault the Imperial cavalry, breaking Hagen's regiment.

11.30AM–12.00PM: Croat horse, panicked by the rapid advance of Bernhard's wing, fall back through their own cavalry, disordering Hagen's arquebusier regiment.

TO HALLE

BATTLE OF LÜTZEN
16 November 1632, 10.45am–12.30pm
Showing the opening stages of the Swedish assault, up to the arrival of Pappenheim, his counterattack and fatal wounding.

WALLENSTEIN

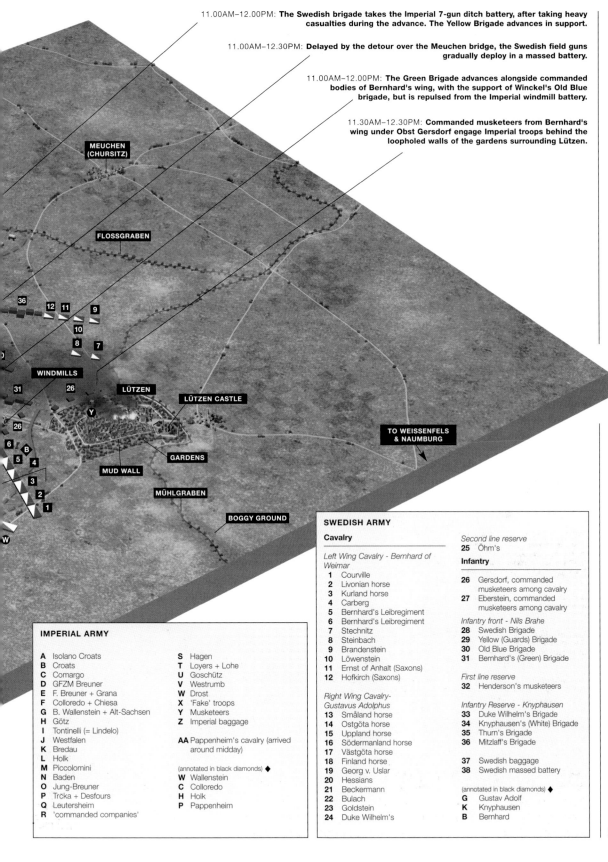

11.00AM–12.00PM: The Swedish brigade takes the Imperial 7-gun ditch battery, after taking heavy casualties during the advance. The Yellow Brigade advances in support.

11.00AM–12.30PM: Delayed by the detour over the Meuchen bridge, the Swedish field guns gradually deploy in a massed battery.

11.00AM–12.00PM: The Green Brigade advances alongside commanded bodies of Bernhard's wing, with the support of Winckel's Old Blue brigade, but is repulsed from the Imperial windmill battery.

11.30AM–12.30PM: Commanded musketeers from Bernhard's wing under Obst Gersdorf engage Imperial troops behind the loopholed walls of the gardens surrounding Lützen.

MEUCHEN (CHURSITZ)

FLOSSGRABEN

WINDMILLS

LÜTZEN

LÜTZEN CASTLE

TO WEISSENFELS & NAUMBURG

GARDENS

MUD WALL

MÜHLGRABEN

BOGGY GROUND

IMPERIAL ARMY

A	Isolano Croats	S	Hagen
B	Croats	T	Loyers + Lohe
C	Comargo	U	Goschütz
D	GFZM Breuner	V	Westrumb
E	F. Breuner + Grana	W	Drost
F	Colloredo + Chiesa	X	'Fake' troops
G	B. Wallenstein + Alt-Sachsen	Y	Musketeers
H	Götz	Z	Imperial baggage
I	Tontinelli (= Lindelo)		
J	Westfalen	**AA**	Pappenheim's cavalry (arrived around midday)
K	Bredau		
L	Holk		
M	Piccolomini	(annotated in black diamonds) ◆	
N	Baden	W	Wallenstein
O	Jung-Breuner	C	Colloredo
P	Trčka + Desfours	H	Holk
Q	Leutersheim	P	Pappenheim
R	'commanded companies'		

SWEDISH ARMY

Cavalry

Left Wing Cavalry - Bernhard of Weimar
1 Courville
2 Livonian horse
3 Kurland horse
4 Carberg
5 Bernhard's Leibregiment
6 Bernhard's Leibregiment
7 Stechnitz
8 Steinbach
9 Brandenstein
10 Löwenstein
11 Ernst of Anhalt (Saxons)
12 Hofkirch (Saxons)

Right Wing Cavalry- Gustavus Adolphus
13 Småland horse
14 Ostgöta horse
15 Uppland horse
16 Södermanland horse
17 Västgöta horse
18 Finland horse
19 Georg v. Uslar
20 Hessians
21 Beckermann
22 Bulach
23 Goldstein
24 Duke Wilhelm's

Second line reserve
25 Öhm's

Infantry
26 Gersdorf, commanded musketeers among cavalry
27 Eberstein, commanded musketeers among cavalry

Infantry front - Nils Brahe
28 Swedish Brigade
29 Yellow (Guards) Brigade
30 Old Blue Brigade
31 Bernhard's (Green) Brigade

First line reserve
32 Henderson's musketeers

Infantry Reserve - Knyphausen
33 Duke Wilhelm's Brigade
34 Knyphausen's (White) Brigade
35 Thurn's Brigade
36 Mitzlaff's Brigade

37 Swedish baggage
38 Swedish massed battery

(annotated in black diamonds) ◆
G Gustav Adolf
K Knyphausen
B Bernhard

57

In his front line Bernhard had at his disposal the best of the German horse, including a number of veteran regiments that had been with Gustav Adolf in Poland. This cavalry was again 'interlined' with five musketeer detachments stiffened with pairs of regimental guns, under the overall command of Oberst Gersdorf. Supporting the attack was the infantry of Duke Bernhard's Green Brigade, and (according to Fleetwood), Winckel's Blue Brigade.[7]

At first Bernhard's advance met with success. The clouds of smoke billowing from Lützen allowed him to approach the roadside ditches relatively unscathed by musketry and cannon fire. The Croat screen fled backwards and Gersdorf's musketeer detachments and regimental guns made short work of the musketeers in the ditches. A fierce engagement began around the heavily fortified miller's house.

One of the largest units on the Imperial right was Hagen's harquebusier regiment, which included a number of raw companies that had yet to be mustered and issued standards. The appearance of the Croats fleeing from out of the smoke unsettled Hagen's panicky recruits, who opened their ranks to let them through. Once disordered, they were easy meat for Bernhard's cavaliers, who charged them, broke up the regiment, relieved them of the few standards they possessed, and sent them fleeing back to the Imperial rear 'in great confusion'. Here they halted with their one remaining standard, and began ignoring repeated orders to return to their original post behind Trčka's cuirassiers.

Fortunately for Wallenstein his other cavalry stood firm, obeying his instructions to take the first enemy charge at the halt. Bernhard's cavalry attack lost momentum and the breakthrough was soon halted. Meanwhile musketry from the walled gardens around Lützen and the miller's house and cannon fire from the windmill battery had beaten back the Protestant infantry. Bernhard's first attack slowly began to fall apart.

The casualties on both sides were heavy. The highest-ranking Imperial loss was the Prince-Abbot of Fulda, Johann Schenk zu Schweinsberg, a Benedictine monk and Prince of the Empire. Evicted from his lands by the Swedes after Breitenfeld, he had obtained Wallenstein's permission to follow the army after declaring his willingness to put up with the 'fare of the humblest soldier'. He was riding from squadron to squadron, blessing and calling them to fight for the Catholic faith, getting increasingly excited by the clamour of battle. Having heard that Pappenheim's troops had arrived, he rode off to find them, only to run into a squadron which he thought was friendly. He rode to its head, was recognised by his priestly habit, and was immediately pistolled dead.

Ottavio Piccolomini (1599–1656). It is now difficult to disentangle Wallenstein's subordinates from the characters in Schiller's novel *Wallenstein*, completed in 1799. Schiller greatly exaggerated the sinister reputation of this Italian aristocrat from a family that had spawned popes. Piccolomini, the former commander of Wallenstein's Lifeguard, later rose to dizzy heights but was a mere colonel at Lützen, though his extraordinary feats led many historians to imagine that he commanded the entire Imperial left wing. Piccolomini was undoubtedly, to borrow a sporting phrase, the 'man of the match'.

PAPPENHEIM ARRIVES, 12.00–12.30PM

Pappenheim arrived on the Imperial left wing 'at about 12', just as it was threatening to disintegrate. There is enough to indicate that he came along the direct route from Halle, without making a detour along the wider road via Leipzig.[8] Accompanying him were three cavalry regiments: Sparr's (under Obstlt Albrecht von Hofkirchen), Bönninghausen's and Lamboy's, along with a few companies of dragoons and Croats and

Johann Graf von Götz (1599–1645). After starting his career in Protestant service, he switched sides in 1626 and raised one the Imperial army's finest cuirassier regiments. At the time of the battle he was in the process of selling the regiment to the Emperor's 19-year-old nephew, Mattias de' Medici, Duke of Florence. (Portrait from Khevenhüller's, *Conterfet Kupfferstich ...*)

Pappenheim's own lifeguard company or *Rennfahne* – in all about 1,500–2,000 horse. Wallenstein informed him of the dire situation on the left flank, which Stålhandske was threatening to turn, and instructed him to intervene.

Pappenheim's appearance on the faltering Imperial left restored order there. The baggage wagons and drivers that had not already disappeared towards Leipzig, were halted and sent to a safer location behind the Imperial right. The Croats rallied and, reinforced by more Croats from Pappenheim's corps, were sent off on a wide outflanking move of the Swedish left. Never one to worry for his own safety (it was widely known that he carried 100 battle scars), Pappenheim personally led the main counter-attack.

Charging forward 'with great fury', Pappenheim was greeted by a salvo from the commanded musketeers and regimental guns accompanying Stålhandske's cavalry. As his personal trumpeter, the 22-year-old Conrad Ehinger, later related: 'The [Count's] lifeguard-company took great damage, and the Count himself was hit by a falconet round[9] and three musket balls.' When Pappenheim slumped from his saddle, the Imperial counter-attack immediately collapsed.

Swedish horsemen milled about the stricken field marshal. His trumpeter begged Obstlt Hofkirchen to advance to his aid, to no avail. In the end he rushed in himself and brought his master away. Seeing a regiment fleeing close by, Pappenheim asked whose they were. 'Bönninghausen's' came the reply, one of his own units. It was too much; tearfully Pappenheim tried to wrench himself up to rejoin the fight, slapping his hands in frustration and shouting at them: 'Ach my brothers, may God have mercy on you! Will not one of you still fight loyally for the Emperor?'

The trumpeter placed his master in a coach. Pappenheim took off his ring, kissed it, and asked him give it to his wife. He left a farewell message to Wallenstein and died in his trumpeter's arms before the coach reached Leipzig. It was later claimed that Pappenheim smiled at the news that the Swedish King had been killed before he himself passed away; this was merely hearsay, an attempt to make sense of the sudden, almost random, death of one of history's great captains.

Piccolomini counter-attacks, 12.00–12.30pm

On the Imperial left-centre, things were not going well for the Imperialists. Wallenstein had instructed Holk to take the first charge at the halt (*à pied ferme*), his plan being to defend the line of the Leipzig road. The Swedish Brigade and the commanded musketeers of the Swedish right wing had managed to push the Imperialists back off the ditches, and they were now beginning to pour salvoes at the infantry and cavalry of the Imperial line.

Obeying Wallenstein's instructions Piccolomini's cavalry stood rigidly still, in full view of two of Eberstein's musketeer detachments, who began firing into them from the safety of the ditches. For 15 minutes the fire continued, killing 'innumerable soldiers and officers'. Emboldened by their success, one of the detachments came forward to fire from just 20 paces. Ottavio's nephew, Rittmeister Silvio Piccolomini, claimed the regiment was only saved from obliteration 'by the blessed Madonna and their cuirasses of proof' [pistol-proof breastplates]. Eventually

THE WINDMILL BATTERY
The main Imperial battery of about 14 guns was positioned near a group of windmills at the right flank of the infantry and was the most heavily entrenched part of Wallenstein's line. Duke Bernhard made repeated assaults on the battery and the nearby miller's house. Twice his men got up to the guns, only to be driven back by Imperial infantry and cavalry posted to the rear of the battery. Only towards the end of the battle, with darkness falling, did the battery finally fall. (Graham Turner)

Franz Albrecht, Duke of Sachsen-Lauenburg (1598–1642) was the highest-ranking member of Gustav Adolf's entourage during his fatal ride. He had since 1625 been colonel of one of the Imperial army's finest cuirassier regiments (Neu-Sachsen, afterwards given to Hatzfeld), and in January 1632 had been sent to the Saxon court to negotiate on Wallenstein's behalf. He resigned from Imperial service during the Nuremberg siege, but because of his cowardly behaviour at Lützen was never hired into the Swedish Army. (*Theatrum Europaeum*, vol. IV, 1st edition)

Piccolomini decided he could take no more: he charged the musketeers and threw them back, but could not follow because of the ditches, and finally decided to retire to a safer position.

In the meantime Götz's cuirassiers, to Piccolomini's right, had attempted to charge the Swedish brigade frontally. The Swedish brigade stood firm and delivered a musket salvo which sent Götz's men reeling back for cover. It seems that soon after this incident the Swedish Brigade, having taken crippling casualties in the initial attack on the ditch battery, was beaten back or withdrawn from the ditch position, but the details are unclear. It was into this morass of milling Imperial cavalry and Swedish infantry under pressure that Gustav Adolf would ride for the last time.

The Death of Gustav Adolf, 12.30–1.00pm

Further to the Swedish right Gustav Adolf had been struggling to find a crossing point over the roadside ditches. He eventually found a narrow grass path which could only be passed in single file, and began crossing along with the Smålanders. Seeing the turmoil to his left (albeit unclearly because of the dense smoke), with Götz's and Piccolomini's cavalry threatening his infantry, Gustav Adolf decided not to wait for his remaining squadrons, the Uppland and Ostgöta horse, but to intervene immediately at the head of his Smålanders.[10]

It was, of course, not the King's place to risk his life by personally leading an attack, but there were unusual circumstances. Stålhandske was with his Finns on the far right, up to a kilometre away; the colonel of the Smålanders, Fredrik Stenbock, had been shot in the foot, and commander of the Östgöta cavalry, Lennart Nilsson Bååt, had been shot fatally in the head: Gustav Adolf was suddenly short of commanders.

Leading forward the Småland horse Gustav Adolf was suddenly struck by a bullet, which grazed the neck of his horse, Streiff, and broke his left arm just above the elbow 'completely in two'. The attack proceeded without him, and he fell back with his entourage of six to eight persons. Meanwhile Piccolomini's horse cut clean through the Smålanders, and sent them scurrying back for the cover of the ditch.

Soon after the battle a theory circulated that Duke Franz Albrecht of Sachsen-Lauenburg, a former Imperialist colonel, had assassinated the Swedish King. He is visible at right centre of this fanciful 19th-century engraving, with a smoking pistol, about to make his getaway.

'How the King of Sweden was killed' by Pierre van der Aa after *Theatrum Europaeum*, vol. II. This print, designed within a few years of the battle, conveys well the circumstances of the King's fatal encounter with a group of heavily armoured Imperial cuirassiers emerging from the smoke.

Separated from the Smålanders in the mist, Gustav Adolf, weakened and in shock, called to Duke Franz Albrecht of Sachsen-Lauenburg to take him out of the action. The royal stablemaster, Von der Schulenburg, took the reins of the King's horse and began to lead him back to the Swedish lines. Suddenly, some of Götz's cuirassiers appeared out of the mist. One of them, distinctive in his burnished steel armour (identified by some as Obstlt Moritz von Falckenberg), recognised the King and called out 'Here's the right bird!' and fired a pistol into the King's back.

The Swedish King's mount, Streiff, was named after a German cavalry colonel, Johann Streiff von Lauenstein, who in 1631 procured it for the King for 1,000 Imperial thalers. The horse died early in 1633, probably from wounds received at Lützen, its hide accompanied the King's body to Stockholm, and was later stuffed and put on exhibition in the Livrustkammaren, where it remains today.

BATTLE OF LÜTZEN

16 November 1632, 12.30pm–3.00pm

Showing the battle at its height, including the death of Gustav Adolf, the Fahnenflucht, destruction of the Blue and Yellow Swedish brigades and the panic in the Swedish rear.

GUSTAV ADO[LF]

XXXX

2.00PM: **Knyphausen sends forwards fresh troops (incl. Thurn's Brigade) to retake the ditch battery.**

12.30–1.00PM: **After finding a crossing place over the Leipzig road, Gustav Adolf leads his cavalry forward to attack, but is hit in the arm by a random shot. Detached from his Småland horse in this mist, he is killed by men of Götz's and Piccolomini's regiments.**

12.30–2.00PM: **Bulach's three squadrons defeat the Croat horse attempting to turn the Swedish flank.**

12.30–1.00PM: **Badly damaged, the Swedish brigade falls back from the ditch battery.**

WOOD

1.00–2.00PM: **Hearing of the King's fate, Stålhandske abandons the assault on the Imperial left and returns to search for the King's body.**

TO LEIPZIG

A

24

23

22

21 20 19 33

28

15 13 32
14 G 27

27 30

M C N 29

H D E K

I J C

18 17 16 O

27 27 27 U R

S

1.00–1.30PM: **After heavy casualties Comargo's regiment combines with Baden's regiment, and returns to its original position, where it is instrumental in the destruction of the Blue Brigade.**

AA2

AA3

Z

H

1.00–1.30PM: **The Blue Brigade, coming up to relieve the Swedish brigade and to lend support to the Yellow brigade, is pinned frontally by the Comargo-Baden brigade and charged in the flank by cuirassiers.**

B

12.45–1.15PM: **The Yellow brigade attacks the Imperial centre, but is 'completely overthrown' by three Imperial brigades.**

Having fallen back from the Imperial right wing, Hagen's disordered regiment refuses repeated orders to return to its original position behind Trcka's regiment.

1.00PM: **Sparr's regiment (under Obstlt. Albrecht v. Hofkirchen) refuses to engage the enemy, and instead moves to the Imperial right rear.**

AA1

2.30PM: **Holk gathers all he can find in the rear areas and attacks, relieving the pressure on Wallenstein, defeating Bernhard's cavalry and swinging the course of this phase of the battle.**

TO HALLE

2.00PM: **Horsemen from Bönninghausen's regiment rout down the Halle road, and inform Reinach's infantry that the battle is lost.**

XXXX

WALLENST[EIN]

1.00–2.30PM: **In his second phase of assaults Bernhard succeeds in turning the Imperial right flank, and almost surrounds Wallenstein.**

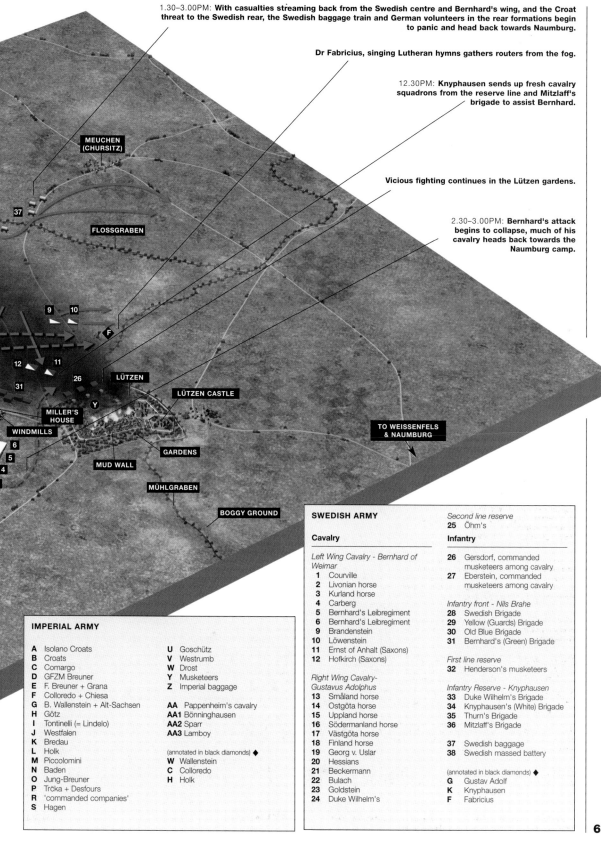

1.30–3.00PM: With casualties streaming back from the Swedish centre and Bernhard's wing, and the Croat threat to the Swedish rear, the Swedish baggage train and German volunteers in the rear formations begin to panic and head back towards Naumburg.

Dr Fabricius, singing Lutheran hymns gathers routers from the fog.

12.30PM: Knyphausen sends up fresh cavalry squadrons from the reserve line and Mitzlaff's brigade to assist Bernhard.

Vicious fighting continues in the Lützen gardens.

2.30–3.00PM: Bernhard's attack begins to collapse, much of his cavalry heads back towards the Naumburg camp.

MEUCHEN (CHURSITZ)

37

FLOSSGRABEN

9 10

F

12 11

31 26

LÜTZEN

LÜTZEN CASTLE

MILLER'S HOUSE

WINDMILLS

Y

6

5

4

GARDENS

MUD WALL

MÜHLGRABEN

BOGGY GROUND

TO WEISSENFELS & NAUMBURG

IMPERIAL ARMY

A	Isolano Croats	U	Goschütz
B	Croats	V	Westrumb
C	Comargo	W	Drost
D	GFZM Breuner	Y	Musketeers
E	F. Breuner + Grana	Z	Imperial baggage
F	Colloredo + Chiesa		
G	B. Wallenstein + Alt-Sachsen	AA	Pappenheim's cavalry
H	Götz	AA1	Bönninghausen
I	Tontinelli (= Lindelo)	AA2	Sparr
J	Westfalen	AA3	Lamboy
K	Bredau		
L	Holk		(annotated in black diamonds) ◆
M	Piccolomini	W	Wallenstein
N	Baden	C	Colloredo
O	Jung-Breuner	H	Holk
P	Trčka + Desfours		
R	'commanded companies'		
S	Hagen		

SWEDISH ARMY

Cavalry

Left Wing Cavalry - Bernhard of Weimar
1 Courville
2 Livonian horse
3 Kurland horse
4 Carberg
5 Bernhard's Leibregiment
6 Bernhard's Leibregiment
9 Brandenstein
10 Löwenstein
11 Ernst of Anhalt (Saxons)
12 Hofkirch (Saxons)

Right Wing Cavalry- Gustavus Adolphus
13 Småland horse
14 Ostgöta horse
15 Uppland horse
16 Södermanland horse
17 Västgöta horse
18 Finland horse
19 Georg v. Uslar
20 Hessians
21 Beckermann
22 Bulach
23 Goldstein
24 Duke Wilhelm's

Second line reserve
25 Öhm's

Infantry

26 Gersdorf, commanded musketeers among cavalry
27 Eberstein, commanded musketeers among cavalry

Infantry front - Nils Brahe
28 Swedish Brigade
29 Yellow (Guards) Brigade
30 Old Blue Brigade
31 Bernhard's (Green) Brigade

First line reserve
32 Henderson's musketeers

Infantry Reserve - Knyphausen
33 Duke Wilhelm's Brigade
34 Knyphausen's (White) Brigade
35 Thurn's Brigade
36 Mitzlaff's Brigade

37 Swedish baggage
38 Swedish massed battery

(annotated in black diamonds) ◆
G Gustav Adolf
K Knyphausen
F Fabricius

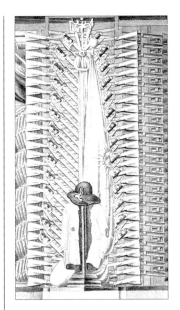

Von der Schulenburg immediately placed his pistol under the lip of the horseman's breastplate and shot him. The 'man who killed Gustavus' would never be able to brag about the fact.

The King had slumped from his horse. His bodyguard, Anders Jönsson, tried to protect him but was cut down. The 18-year-old page Augustus Leubelfing turned back to offer the King his own horse, but was also fatally wounded. The King took several rapier thrusts through his body. Outnumbered by cuirassiers, the rest of the royal entourage fled for their lives. One of the cuirassiers asked the name of the stricken cavalier. Gustav Adolf is said to have replied 'I was the King of Sweden.' When a body of Swedish horse approached, someone delivered the coup de grâce with a pistol shot in the temple.

One of Piccolomini's men, a certain Innocentius Bucela, had recognised the fallen King and soon after directed Piccolomini to the body, which was 'still quivering'. Piccolomini's soldiers removed the famous buffcoat, Holk's trumpeter got one of the spurs, another soldier pocketed the royal signet ring. Piccolomini considered taking the body

The full unravelling of the circumstances of Gustav Adolf's death was made possible by the return to Sweden of the one piece of evidence that was incontestable – the King's buffcoat. Having been on exhibition in Vienna throughout the 18th and 19th centuries it was handed back by the Austrian government after World War I in gratitude for the work of the Swedish Red Cross. The buffcoat and damaged hat (which also fell into Wallenstein's hands but has since disappeared), are shown here on display in Vienna in 1817. (After Cederström, *Gustav Adolf II vid Lützen*)

RIGHT **Gustav Adolf was unable to wear metal armour because of a musket wound in the neck received in Poland, and relied entirely on an elk-skin buffcoat made for him by an Englishman. Forensic study of the buffcoat has given detailed data of the pistol shots and rapier thrusts inflicted on the King. The sword (a German model with Solingen blade, signed 'Marson') and pistols (of Netherlands manufacture c.1620) are also regarded as Lützen mementoes, but are perhaps just objects owned by the King. (Livrustkammaren, Stockholm)**

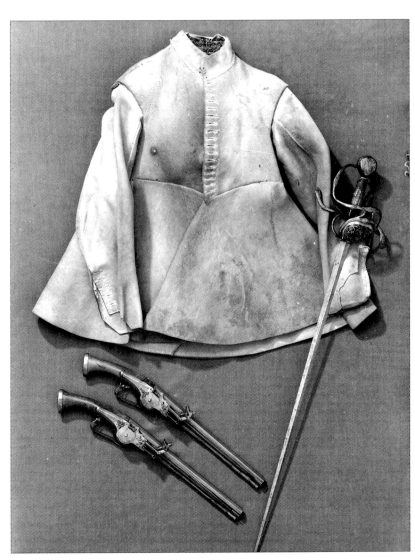

from the field, but the appearance of another troop of Swedish horse, looking for their King, forced him to retire.

Destruction of the Yellow & Blue brigades, 12.30–1.30pm

In that confused hour that saw the deaths of Gustav Adolf and Pappenheim on the right wing, nightmarish scenes were unfolding in the centre. After being pushed back from the Imperial ditch battery, the Swedes launched a second assault, this time directed more towards the Imperial centre. Brahe led forward his own brigade, the Yellow Brigade, the bulk of which was formed from the elite Yellow or Court Regiment. The King's orders to Count Nils Brahe had been quite specific: 'To go boldly at the enemy and not take heed of their numbers, nor to fire any salvoes until the Imperial musketeers had fired themselves.'

The orders were carried out to the letter. The Yellow Brigade marched solemnly up towards the enemy without firing. The idea was to tempt the enemy into discharging their muskets first. Armoured pikemen advanced at the head of the brigade, hoping to shield their own musketeers from the worst of the enemy discharge. Once the enemy had fired, the musketeers would be able to march up with impunity, delivering their 'Swedish salvo' at just 5 to 10 paces, before charging in. It was a monumental game of 'chicken'. The 'salvo' tactic had worked in the past, but this time facing the Yellow Brigade was not one, but three Imperial brigades, all veterans. The Imperial quartermaster-general, Giulio Diodati (probably from the vantage point of Grana's regiment, of which he was also oberstleutnant), watched the calm approach of the Yellow Brigade in amazement: 'A great body with yellow casacks [coats] came up resolutely in formation and with pikes covering their musketeers. When attacked by our infantry, the body was completely overthrown, and it was a wonder to see in a moment the body reduced to a mound of corpses.'

The Imperial brigades had indeed been tempted to fire first, but at point-blank range. The Imperial salvo instantly felled many Swedish officers, who usually led the pike bodies. Count Brahe was shot just above the right knee; several captains went down, including Monro's friend, the Scotsman Henry Lindsay of Bainshow, 'hurt with the Cannon, and musket twice … who for a time did lie almost dead in the field.' Paralysed by the losses, the brigade was unable to deploy to return fire.

Worse was to come.

While the advance of the Yellow Brigade had been brought to an abrupt halt, the Blue Brigade had come up on its flank, in place of the mangled Swedish Brigade. The Brigade was made up of a single unit, the Old Blue Regiment, one of Gustav Adolf's largest and most experienced German units, which had been raised in 1624. The march of the Blue Brigade took it across the ditches, and directly at one of Tilly's oldest Walloon regiments, Comargo's, formed in 1619. Comargo's regiment had already suffered heavy casualties: Theodor Comargo himself had been shot four times, and his lieutenant colonel was dead. The senior surviving officer was Oberst-wachtmeister Hans von Münchhausen.[11] Münchhausen had combined his depleted unit with one from the second line – Baden's regiment (whose colonel was absent and lieutenant colonel was dead) and set a trap for the Blue Brigade.

Nils Brahe Count of Visingsborg (1604–32), scion of one of Sweden's top families, had already, aged 28, risen to General-major of infantry and held the colonelcy of the prestigious Yellow or Court Regiment (Hofregiment). Gustav Adolf considered him more talented than his soon-to-be-famous artillery commander Lennart Torstensson, and was nursing him for the highest echelons of command. (Rydboholm, Sweden)

DESTRUCTION OF THE OLD BLUE BRIGADE
Shortly after the King's death the elite Blue Brigade advanced at the Imperial centre, straight into some of Wallenstein's best troops. Pinned by Comargo's Infantry Regiment to its front, the Brigade was charged in the flank by Imperial cuirassiers. The veterans fought stolidly, holding their ground, 'as if they'd forgotten how to retreat', but were overwhelmed, leaving the greater part of their number lying as if in a great mound. (Graham Turner)

Sheltering behind them, out of sight, were five companies of Imperial cuirassiers.

Münchhausen watched as the Blue Brigade approached in its characteristic triangular formation, looking like 'three regiments all clumped together'. Once the firefight began and the Swedes were pinned, the cavalry charged on both flanks at once. The carnage was worse than that inflicted on the Yellow Brigade. Oberst Winckel was wounded, along with his lieutenant colonel, Caspar Wolff, and the regiment lost most of its flags. Münchhausen later presented Wallenstein with 15 colours, of which Comargo's regiment alone took ten. Münchhausen believed there were 'over 2000 enemy dead on the place'.

Watts summed up the destruction of the Yellow and Blue brigades in heroic terms: 'These 2 brigades were of the flower of the Army: old souldiers of 7 or 8 yeeres service (the most of them) and whom the King had there placed, for that he most relied on them … their dead bodies now covered the same ground, which living they had defended. These were old beaten souldiers, indeed, but it was so long since they had beene last beaten, that they had by this time forgotten how to runne away.'

The Swedish assault in the centre had ended in utter disaster: in a few minutes Gustav Adolf's best infantry regiments, the pride of his army, had been all but wiped out.

IMPERIAL WINGS IN TURMOIL

The *Fahnenflucht*, 12.30–1.30pm

Fortunately for the Swedes, the Imperialists were unable to take advantage of their success in the centre. Smoke shrouded the field, and few officers could see beyond their neighbouring formations. The Imperial centre had also taken heavy casualties, and was under fire from the Swedish main battery. Rather than pursue the enemy, the Imperialists followed Wallenstein's order to hold their ground; after rallying and plugging the holes in their formations, they resumed their allotted slots in the line behind the Leipzig road.

An advance was inappropriate in view of the crisis unfolding on both Imperial wings. Pappenheim had fallen in full view of his regiments (unlike Gustav Adolf who had disappeared in thick smoke), and the morale of his men had collapsed. Sparr's regiment, led by Obstlt Albrecht von Hofkirchen, became disordered and fell back. After rallying Hofkirchen switched wings, in the mistaken view that the Imperial right was a safer location. When Bernhard's troops threatened to turn the Imperial right, Hofkirchen refused a direct personal order from Wallenstein to attack, and fell back once again. Meanwhile Bönninghausen's regiment fell apart. Several companies of his regiment left the field along with their officers and standards, and at about 2.00pm encountered Pappenheim's infantry on the march from Halle, telling them the battle was lost.

ABOVE, LEFT **Gustav Adolf's own infantry lifeguard (or drabant) company fought as part of the Yellow Brigade and shared its fate. Their black silk flag, described on this 17th-century watercolour by Möhner as 'His Royal Majesty's Life Colours' and in *The Swedish Intelligencer* as the 'Standard Royall', was lost during the action. (For a reconstruction see Men-at-Arms 235: *The Army of Gustavus Adolphus (1) Infantry*, Plate F).**

Lohe's cuirassiers, which had been in this post before Pappenheim's arrival, also fell back after their colonel was killed. Scant few troops remained on the Imperial left to withstand Stålhandske's attack, but somehow Holk managed to hold things together. Then, at the critical point, Stålhandske heard of the King's death and suddenly the pressure eased.

Bernhard's second assault, 1.00–3.00pm

Shortly after 1.00pm, Bernhard launched a second phase of assaults on the Imperial right wing. His first attack had taken heavy casualties; now he asked Knyphausen to release reserves. Knyphausen duly fed forward cavalry squadrons from the second line, among them Prince Ernst of Anhalt's, Brandenstein's and Löwenstein's regiments plus Mitzlaff's infantry brigade. The Swedish field artillery had now arrived and was formed into a 'grand battery', facing the Imperial centre and mills. With these fresh forces at his disposal, Bernhard led forward a more determined and vigorous attack on the Imperial right wing.

The walled gardens ringing Lützen were the key to the wing. Flanking fire from their loopholed walls could disorder any Swedes who attempted to advance through the narrow gap between the town and windmills. Oberst Gersdorf's commanded musketeers and their supporting regimental guns again went forward to clear the gardens, in one of the most furious contests of the battle. In one of these attacks Gersdorf was himself killed.

Bernhard's cavalry pushed forward and this time their greater numbers began to tell; the Imperial horse began to fall back. The cavalry action became especially desperate, with Trčka's and Holk's cuirassiers in the thick of the mêlée. The wing had been seriously weakened by the rout of Hagen's regiment, which now dawdled in the rear near Goschütz's regiment, in 'no good order', ignoring repeated calls to return to its original position. In the death sentence later handed down to Hagen, it was stated that his cowardice was a major contribution to the partial breaking of the right wing 'which probably if [Hagen] had complied with his orders and charged along with the other [horse] units, or at least joined them, would never have happened'. Wallenstein had personally to cover for Hagen, and made sure he got no mercy.

Indeed it was here on the Imperial right and at the mills that Wallenstein spent most of the battle, riding from regiment to regiment, realising that the action would be decided here. Accompanying him was a throng of staff officers and volunteers, all hoping he would witness their valour. Among them was Count Otto Friedrich von Harrach, Wallenstein's chamberlain and brother of his wife, Isabella. Harrach was not far from Wallenstein when he was hit by a musket ball, which entered near the throat and exited through his ear. This 'brave cavalier' slumped from his horse and was ridden over several times, but somehow was able

ABOVE **A satin doublet belonging to Count Nils Brahe, said to have been worn at Lützen, where he was fatally wounded in the thigh while leading an infantry attack on the Imperial centre. Brahe died on 1 December. (Bielke Armoury, Skokloster)**

ABOVE, RIGHT **A gilded silver finial said to be from Gustav Adolf's 'life standard'. In 1945 this object (surviving length 11.5cm) was in the collection of an Italian contessa living near Udine, Italy. It was no doubt acquired by one of Wallenstein's Italian officers who took it from the King's lifeguard at Lützen.**

LEFT **Hans Georg aus dem Winckel, Oberst of the 'Old Blue' infantry regiment. He received two wounds to his left arm at Lützen, just above the elbow and in the hand. This engraving of him was made in Augsburg in 1634 while he was governor of the city. (Uppsala University Library)**

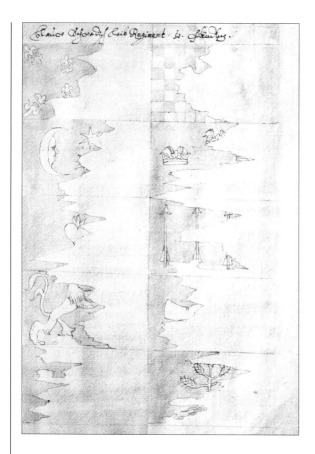

to get up and retire from the field, and survived the experience. Even more keen to impress were Emperor Ferdinand's two teenage nephews, Mattias and Francesco de' Medici, Princes of Tuscany and Dukes of Florence, sons of Grand Duke Cosimo II. 'They were keen to be everywhere and see everything of interest' noted Diodati. One of the young princes had a lucky escape when a cannonball killed the horse under him, narrowly missing his thigh.

The fire was not all one way. The 24-year-old Prince Ernst of Anhalt, son of Christian, the commander of the Bohemians at White Mountain, was fatally wounded at the head of his Saxon cavalry regiment. Meanwhile the Green Brigade, shattered by the intensity of the Imperial barrage, took shelter from the windmill battery behind the rubble of the miller's house.

On the whole though, things seemed to be going well for Bernhard, his cavalry were beginning to outflank the Imperial right wing. The situation was so serious that, according to Holk, Wallenstein was almost completely surrounded. But Holk had been busy in the rear areas, rallying Pappenheim's men, and gathering together any other troops he could find. Now that Stålhandske

ABOVE **Colours of the 'Blue Swedish Life Regiment'. Opinion is divided on whether they belonged to the 'Old Blue' mercenary regiment or to a Swedish national regiment: most evidence suggests the former. Nearly all the Old Blue Regiment's flags fell into Imperial hands at Lützen, but they were so tatty, remarked Diodati, that it was not worth sending them as trophies to the Emperor. These watercolours painted by the Augsburg cleric Reginbaldus Möhner have faded with age; the original shades were mid-blue with yellow devices. (Archiv des Bischoflichen Ordinariat, Augsburg)**

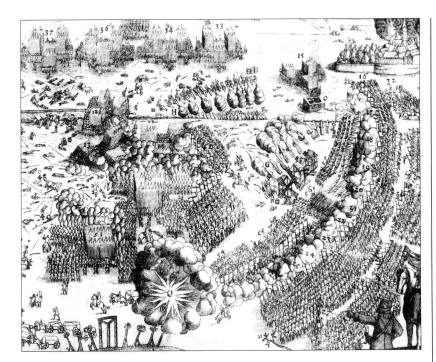

had ceased to attack, Holk had the breathing space he needed. His advance at the head of these reserves, in the nick of time, completely changed the course of the action. Bernhard's horse began to fall back and then crumble.

The Swedes on the verge of collapse

Between 1.30 and 2.30pm, the Swedish Army began to fall apart. Two of the four infantry brigades of the front line had been destroyed, the other two were crippled. The Swedish right wing had been paralysed by the King's disappearance. The attack of Bernhard's wing, successful at first, was beginning to founder.

Contributing to the anxiety that began to envelop the Swedish ranks was a Croat outflanking attack, set in motion earlier on Pappenheim's initiative. The Croats numbered at least 1,000 horse, and perhaps twice that. Swinging far to the east beyond the Flossgraben and near the Schkölzig Wood, they now emerged in a position directly threatening the Swedish rear.

The three outermost squadrons of the Swedish rear line under Bulach, sent earlier to 'imp out the feathers' of the right wing, set to work. The action was fierce and bloody: several Swedish standards were lost and Obstlt Rehlinger commanding Goldstein's regiment was shot in the arm. In the end, the Croats were pushed back and do not seem to have got anywhere near the Swedish baggage, but their cruel reputation preceded them. Many of the Swedish drivers turned their wagons about and headed back in panic towards Naumburg, taking with them much of the army provisions and ammunition. Even the King's empty carriage joined the chaotic retreat.

Confusion and rumour spread, and members of the Swedish field chancellery, civilian observers and cavalrymen from the rear squadrons began to stream back towards Naumburg. Duke Bernhard's older and more sombre brother, Duke Ernst, then commanding a section of the

Eigentliche Abbildung der Zwischen NAUMBVRG vnd

Weg nach Naumburg

König aus Schwe:
den bleibt
Thot.

The Swedish routers who fled on the 'Weg nach (road to) Naumburg' included infantry from the devastated centre brigades and horsemen from both wings, their escape assisted by the dense smog. (Detail from the broadsheet: Eigentliche Abbildung der Zwischen Naumburg und Lützenam 15. 16. und 17. Novembris 1632 ergangener Schlacht, Uppsala University Library, Planer Samling 69)

rear line, watched with disgust as many of the 'happy-go-lucky volunteers' disappeared into the fog.

In the middle of the mist was the King's chaplain, Fabricius, who had watched the King cross over a ditch with the Småland regiment, and not long after saw them return without him. His enquiries about the King's whereabouts had been met with silence, until the Småland regimental chaplain replied in Latin: *Rex vulneratus est* (The King is wounded). Riding off to find Gustav Adolf, Fabricius came across musketeers, horsemen and wounded officers streaming to the rear through the ever thickening smog. Two fleeing members of the field chancellery called to him: *Fugiendum est* (It's a rout). He replied, also in Latin, that they must stand, 'otherwise by our flight we will provoke everyone to run'.

Fabricius fell in with a Livonian nobleman, Tiesenhausen (probably commander of the Livonian horse), and an English colonel, Fleetwood, who were shouting at the routers to halt. 'The harder we shouted, the faster they began to hurry away, saying that the enemy was just behind them.' Then came an inspired idea. Fabricius began to sing a Lutheran hymn that no Catholic would ever dream of singing. Before long several hundred Protestant soldiers had emerged out of the mist and joined in. With Fleetwood's help Fabricius convinced them to rejoin the battle.

Knyphausen keeps his cool

The Swedish Army was now in crisis. Fortunately one of Germany's most experienced officers, Knyphausen, had a firm hand on the Swedish

Dr Jacob Fabricius (1593–1654), court and army chaplain and Gustav Adolf's confidant. Soon after the King's death, with the Swedish Army beginning to collapse, Fabricius sang Lutheran hymns to provide a rallying point in the thick smoke of battle. Portrait by Lucas Kilian, made during the Swedish army's sojourn in Augsburg in 1632.

George Fleetwood (1605–67) was colonel of a newly raised English mercenary regiment stationed in Polish Prussia, and served at Lützen as a volunteer. According to the King's chaplain, Fabricius, he played a key part in rallying the Swedish routers, yet modestly made no mention of this in his account of the battle. (Private collection)

reserve line. Having lived through many earlier Protestant defeats, he was ideally qualified to extract the army from the panic that was beginning to engulf it. Temporarily assuming command of the Swedish right and centre, he steadied the Protestant infantry reserve line by announcing that 'the King is only wounded'. This allowed the shattered remains of the front line to pass through the intervals in the second and to rally behind them.

Knyphausen then pushed forward fresh troops to plug the gap left by Brahe's brigades. Among them was Thurn's brigade, Henderson's musketeers and perhaps several cavalry squadrons of the right rear, including the Hessian horse, who received special mention for their bravery. Soon after 2.00pm the small Imperial battery was retaken, possibly by Henderson's musketeers, who were in possession of it at the end of battle. According to Oberst Dalbier, the guns 'had at first been spiked in haste, but seeing that no attempt was made to retake them, Monsieur Knyphausen commanded the nails to be removed, sending them cannonballs of the correct calibres, and had them play continuously on the enemy'. Dalbier was a close associate of Knyphausen, and had fought alongside him in several earlier campaigns. Having no field command on the day, he seems to have acted as Knyphausen's assistant.[12] These seven cannon of the ditch battery now had a commanding view over the Imperial left and centre. Dalbier noted that their fire was so effective that: 'By about three o'clock no one remained on the left wing of the enemy.'

The Swedish right wing was in no state to exploit the success: the Småland, Uppland and Östgöta cavalry had all fallen back behind the Leipzig road and ditch. The Smålanders knew well of the King's fate: they had seen the King's horse emerge from the mist, riderless, wounded in the neck and with blood over the still-holstered pistols. Their morale was not helped when Duke Franz Albrecht of Sachsen-Lauenburg rode back towards Naumburg taking a large number of horsemen with him.

Command on the right wing devolved on Överste Stålhandske, who at the time of the King's death was out on the far right with his Finns and half of the Swedish horse. On hearing the dreadful news, Stålhandske abandoned his successful assault and took personal charge of the operation to recover the King's body. Towards 3.00pm the body was located, stripped of everything but three shirts, 'rifled and half-naked, and so disfigured with blood and dirt that he could hardly be known'. It was placed on an ammunition wagon provide by the artillery major, Jernlöd, and taken secretively to Meuchen church, where the village pastor administered last rites.

It was also at about 3.00pm that Bernhard's second phase of attacks near the windmills were finally beaten off. His cavalry and infantry had been decimated. His own cavalry regiment and infantry brigade had taken horrendous casualties. Many of his officers, personal friends and drinking companions, were lying face down in the Lützen mud. Others were abandoning the field and heading back towards Naumburg. For all the spilt blood, Bernhard had won barely an inch of ground.

Bernhard had heard rumours of the King's death. Now, at the first opportunity, he went to see if they were true. He approached Knyphausen's position in the centre, 'with scant few of his men', reported Dalbier, 'believing that we had lost the battle'.

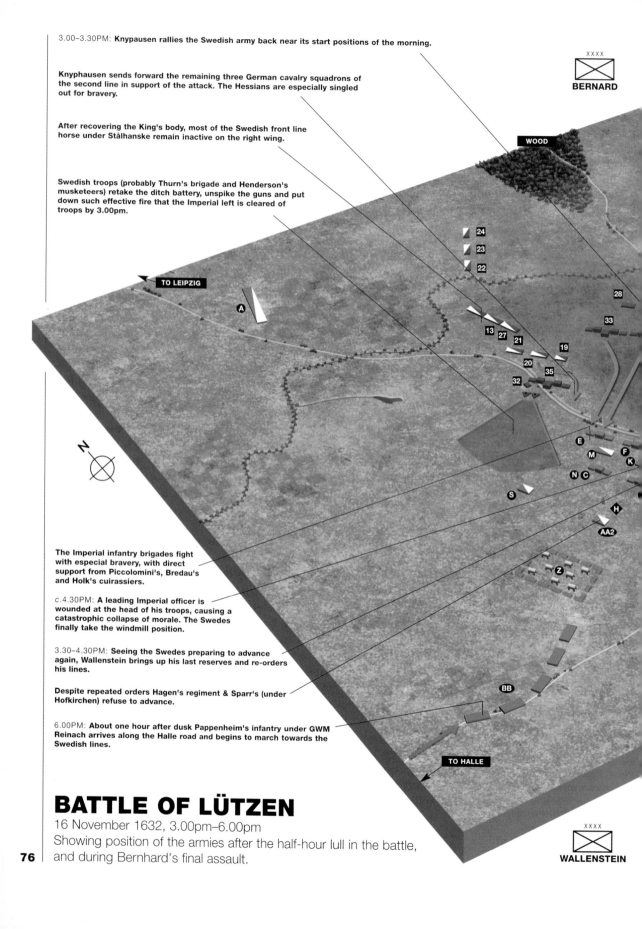

3.00–3.30PM: Knypausen rallies the Swedish army back near its start positions of the morning.

Knyphausen sends forward the remaining three German cavalry squadrons of the second line in support of the attack. The Hessians are especially singled out for bravery.

After recovering the King's body, most of the Swedish front line horse under Stålhanske remain inactive on the right wing.

Swedish troops (probably Thurn's brigade and Henderson's musketeers) retake the ditch battery, unspike the guns and put down such effective fire that the Imperial left is cleared of troops by 3.00pm.

BERNARD

WOOD

TO LEIPZIG

The Imperial infantry brigades fight with especial bravery, with direct support from Piccolomini's, Bredau's and Holk's cuirassiers.

c.4.30PM: A leading Imperial officer is wounded at the head of his troops, causing a catastrophic collapse of morale. The Swedes finally take the windmill position.

3.30–4.30PM: Seeing the Swedes preparing to advance again, Wallenstein brings up his last reserves and re-orders his lines.

Despite repeated orders Hagen's regiment & Sparr's (under Hofkirchen) refuse to advance.

6.00PM: About one hour after dusk Pappenheim's infantry under GWM Reinach arrives along the Halle road and begins to march towards the Swedish lines.

TO HALLE

BATTLE OF LÜTZEN
16 November 1632, 3.00pm–6.00pm
Showing position of the armies after the half-hour lull in the battle, and during Bernhard's final assault.

WALLENSTEIN

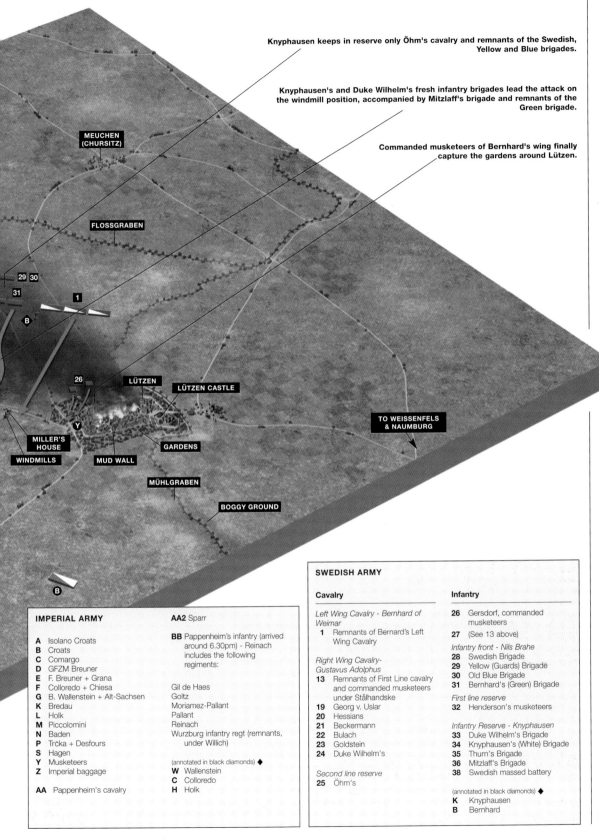

Knyphausen keeps in reserve only Öhm's cavalry and remnants of the Swedish, Yellow and Blue brigades.

Knyphausen's and Duke Wilhelm's fresh infantry brigades lead the attack on the windmill position, accompanied by Mitzlaff's brigade and remnants of the Green brigade.

Commanded musketeers of Bernhard's wing finally capture the gardens around Lützen.

MEUCHEN (CHURSITZ)

FLOSSGRABEN

29 30
31
1
B

26
LÜTZEN
LÜTZEN CASTLE

TO WEISSENFELS & NAUMBURG

Y
MILLER'S HOUSE
WINDMILLS   MUD WALL   GARDENS

MÜHLGRABEN

BOGGY GROUND

B

IMPERIAL ARMY

A Isolano Croats
B Croats
C Comargo
D GFZM Breuner
E F. Breuner + Grana
F Colloredo + Chiesa
G B. Wallenstein + Alt-Sachsen
K Bredau
L Holk
M Piccolomini
N Baden
P Trčka + Desfours
S Hagen
Y Musketeers
Z Imperial baggage

AA Pappenheim's cavalry

AA2 Sparr

BB Pappenheim's infantry (arrived around 6.30pm) - Reinach includes the following regiments:

Gil de Haes
Goltz
Moriamez-Pallant
Pallant
Reinach
Wurzburg infantry regt (remnants, under Willich)

(annotated in black diamonds) ◆
W Wallenstein
C Colloredo
H Holk

SWEDISH ARMY

Cavalry

Left Wing Cavalry - Bernhard of Weimar
1 Remnants of Bernard's Left Wing Cavalry

Right Wing Cavalry- Gustavus Adolphus
13 Remnants of First Line cavalry and commanded musketeers under Stålhandske
19 Georg v. Uslar
20 Hessians
21 Beckermann
22 Bulach
23 Goldstein
24 Duke Wilhelm's

Second line reserve
25 Öhm's

Infantry

26 Gersdorf, commanded musketeers
27 (See 13 above)

Infantry front - Nils Brahe
28 Swedish Brigade
29 Yellow (Guards) Brigade
30 Old Blue Brigade
31 Bernhard's (Green) Brigade

First line reserve
32 Henderson's musketeers

Infantry Reserve - Knyphausen
33 Duke Wilhelm's Brigade
34 Knyphausen's (White) Brigade
35 Thurn's Brigade
36 Mitzlaff's Brigade
38 Swedish massed battery

(annotated in black diamonds) ◆
K Knyphausen
B Bernhard

77

Fortunately, thanks to Knyphausen, the centre was in better shape than Bernhard expected. Knyphausen had jealously guarded a reserve well out of cannon-shot. Two brigades of foot (Knyphausen's own, and Duke Wilhelm's) and Öhm's regiment of horse stood mint and untouched, a stark contrast to the ragged and depleted formations of Bernhard's wing. Behind them, having fallen back through the intervals, shattered, but slowly rallying, were the remnants of the Swedish, Yellow and Blue brigades. Knyphausen had fought strictly by the book, keeping a reserve unengaged to cover a withdrawal.

After confirming that Gustav Adolf was dead, and handing over to Bernhard command of the army, Knyphausen assured him that his troops were in good order and that he could withdraw safely under their cover. There was caution, not cowardice in his advice. Bernhard's spirits lifted, and he declared in stirring phrases that he could not think of retreat, only of dying or winning the battle, 'and of making his revenge as memorable as their loss'.

The Lull 3.00–3.30pm

At about 3.00pm a relative calm descended over the field. At the mills, Colloredo's and Bernhard's men had, as Watts put it, 'fallen off one from another: like two Duellers leaning on their swords, to take breath againe'. And though the artillery batteries continued to pound away, the musket salvoes had died out. The rival armies had, in effect, parted contact.

In this pause, which Watts states lasted half an hour, Knyphausen had sensibly drawn the Protestant lines back out of artillery range, to reorder near their late-morning starting positions. (Watts perhaps exaggerates when he says that they were near the [Schkölzig] wood.)

Bernhard's resolve to continue the battle was mounting. Having reviewed the centre, he rode over to the right wing, finding it 'not in the best circumstances'. With stirring phrases he got the horse squadrons to reassemble for another attack, but not all units responded. The Smålanders had taken heavy casualties and knew better than anyone else the truth about their King. When Bernhard ordered them to follow him, their lieutenant colonel attempted to obstruct him, and Bernhard struck him across the body with the flat of his sword. (Richelieu's memoirs)

In the centre Knyphausen deployed his last reserves, all except Öhm's cavalry regiment, for the renewed attack. The rear infantry line had now, in effect, swapped place with the front line. If the assault failed it could cost dear: according to Watts, the Blue and Yellow Brigades together 'could not make one Squadron strong: which is but the third part of one of them'. They also lacked pikes, which had been broken in combat or dropped during the rout.

As the smoke of battle gradually cleared, it seemed from the Swedish lines that the Imperialists had all but vanished. Wallenstein's left wing was entirely empty. Only three infantry brigades remained visible behind the breastworks near the windmills. Dalbier saw only two. These brigades were no more than the vanguard of a position that had contracted to avoid the Swedish artillery fire from the captured seven-gun ditch battery. Behind them the Imperialists had fallen back to reorder.

The Imperialists were equally relieved at the cessation of hostilities, but were unsure what was happening. Many of Wallenstein's men had

Friedrich Breuner (1601–38) was a member of a large family from Styria in Austria, no less than three members of which commanded regiments at Lützen. His newly levied regiment was posted in the Imperial front line, brigaded with Grana's veteran regiment.

seen the flight of Bernhard's wing, and (according to the *Spanish Relation*) believed the battle had been won. Much of the Swedish line had disappeared from view. To ascertain their whereabouts Wallenstein sent forward Colonels Trčka and Piccolomini to 'take more exact notice of what was rumour'd'. Before long they returned with ominous news – 'the enemy in full Battell-ray was marching towards us in as good order as the first'.

THE FINAL ASSAULT, 3.30–5.00PM

'When the word was given for a new Charge: "alas Camarade" (said the poore souldiers one to another) "must we fall on againe!" "Come says tother" (embracing him) "Courage; if wee must, lets doe it bravely, and make a day of it".' (Watts)

When Wallenstein realised that another Swedish assault was about to be launched, the Imperial lines were a buzz of activity. Reordered front-line battalions were marshalled forward; musketeers were put into the roadside trenches and suburban gardens; reserve battalions that Holk had been husbanding to the last, along with detachments newly arrived from some outlying outpost, were pushed into the front line. When the Swedes saw these apparently fresh troops advancing, a murmur ran along the line, 'Pappenheim's Foot are come … Pappenheim's Foot are come!' Almost to a man it was believed that Pappenheim's infantry had finally arrived. In reality they were still two to three hours' march down the Halle road.

The volume of fire from the main Swedish field battery increased, and was answered from the windmill battery. Meanwhile soldiers of Bernhard's, Mitzlaff's, Knyphausen's and Duke Wilhelm's infantry brigades stiffened themselves for the fight, and marched forwards. Supporting them were the remnants of the cavalry wings, including a few fresh squadrons from the right rear.

The battle was now re-joined with greater fury and desperation than in the earlier attacks. 'A fatal earnestness was seen and heard on both sides' noted Berlepsch. The musketeers now approached to barely five paces from the enemy before giving fire. The fighting came to push of pike and crunch of musket butt. The din and smoke was terrific. No quarter was asked for, or given. [13]

Once again the Imperial cavalry fought in close cooperation with the foot. Bredau's, Holk's and Trčka's cuirassiers were in the thick of the fray. Wallenstein's brother-in-law, Oberst Adam Trčka, had the heel torn from his boot by a cannonball. Piccolomini seemed to be everywhere, now on his sixth horse, his clothing thick with blood from no less than five musket wounds. His regiment had charged ten times and achieved miracles, but at the loss of nearly all its captains and upwards of 200 troopers killed or wounded.

The wounding of a senior Imperial commander, in full view of his troops, seemed to signal a change in fortune for the Imperialists. 'The losse of this commander soe astonished them all that the officers rann about him, and the soldyers flonge downe their armes and rann awaye, and the officers could by noe meanes make them longer stande.' (Fleetwood) The Swedes speculated that the fallen officer was Colloredo or Merode, perhaps even Pappenheim. In fact nearly *all* the senior officers present were hit. Colloredo, overall commander of the infantry, was grazed in arm and head by musket balls. The generalissimo's relative, Oberst Berthold von Waldstein, was grievously hurt: he had all day commanded the infantry near the mills, 'standing with incredible heartiness at the head of his squadron, until eventually a musket ball hit him in the thigh'. (The wound festered and proved fatal.) Another brigade commander, General-feldzeugmeister Breuner, was hit in the face and killed outright. Almost every front-line brigade lost its colonel or lieutenant colonel. Grana was more fortunate – his armour deflecting several musket balls.

Young Waldstein's and Breuner's regiments took the brunt of the damage, with (according to Watts) 'full half, if not two-thirds of the souldiers' killed during the six long hours of action. Wallenstein himself did not escape unhurt. A musket ball bruised his left thigh, without penetrating the skin. In another incident a Hessian *rittmeister*, Bodo von Bodenhausen, managed to ride within four paces of the generalissimo and loosed a pistol shot, which somehow missed.

The Protestant infantry were no less shattered. The Green Brigade was especially hard hit. Its commander, Oberst Wildenstein, had been killed, along with the oberstleutnant of Bernhard's Leibregiment. Fleetwood noted that Bernhard's regiment could barely muster 50 men in arms. Mitzlaff's infantry brigade also took considerable casualties, and the fresh brigades did not remain unscathed, with the brigade commanders, Oberst Bose and Thurn, both receiving wounds. Of the cavalry regiments, many of which had charged ten times, Bernhard's own (which had charged no less than 15 times), Löwenstein's, Brandenstein's and Ernst of Anhalt's had taken crippling casualties.

As darkness fell, Bernhard's infantry finally made it into the windmill position and took the Imperial guns. It had taken them all day, but nightfall made their sacrifice meaningless.

4   Modern authors have the army awake and assembled two hours before dawn; the eyewitness accounts suggest a more leisurely start.
5   Monro, *His Expedition...* (1637), II, pp.163. Monro uses the term 'Dutch' when he means Germans. I have substituted 'Deutsch'.
6   This would explain Hallenus's comment (based on information from two junior officers of the Swedish Brigade) that Brahe led the 'left wing' of the attack.
7   The movements of the Old Blue and (New) Blue or Swedish Brigade are often confused in the sources. In my reconstruction I have chosen to follow the generally accepted interpretation of events, which requires that the Old Blue replaced the New Blue at the ditch battery at about 1.00pm.
8   Pappenheim's time of arrival was recorded by Holk and Münchhausen, though an account in Richelieu's memoirs (supplied by Bernhard's chancellery) states that he reached the field earlier and Wallenstein had sent him to a quiet area to rest his horses.
9   A falconet was a small-bore cannon, in this context clearly a regimental gun. An anonymous account from Leipzig mentions that Pappenheim was hit by a wire ball (*draht Kugel*). The Swedish engineer Schildknecht commented that regimental gun cartridges were held together with wire.
10   The location of Gustav Adolf's death site has long been debated. The argument took a step backwards when Josef Seidler (see bibliography) proposed that the King died on the Swedish left, near the mills, while coming to the assistance of Bernhard. His ideas, which took liberties with the chronology of the battle, the positioning of units and common sense, were taken up by Michael Roberts and from him have entered the popular literature. The evidence for the King's death occurring on the right, both written and pictorial, is overwhelming.
11   Münchhausen left an important account of the battle (G. Wittrock, *Fyra relationer om slaget vid Lützen*, Historisk Tidskrift, 1932 pp.304-5). This has long been misidentified as by an Imperial cavalry officer – he was in fact a Catholic League infantry officer!
12   Johann Dalbier's unpublished *Relation of the battle of Lützen* (London, Public Records Office, SP81/39/fol. 260+) was the first reliable account of the battle to reach England, but is completely unknown to Swedish and German historians.
13   The only prisoner of consequence taken on the dat was Obstlt Tavigny of Lamboy's Regiment.

AFTER NIGHTFALL

A curious defeat – the Imperial army after dark

By 5.00pm the November darkness had fallen. The cannon fire and musket salvoes, which had been audible 20km away, petered out and an eerie stillness descended over the field. The Imperial army gradually reassembled 'one half English mile' back from the mills. Too exhausted to move, many soldiers slept on the ground. The English cavalry captain Sydenam Poyntz, rested his head on his horse's flank, and both fell asleep.

Pappenheim's infantry under Generalwachtmeister Count Heinrich Reinach began to arrive at about 6.00pm, about an hour after nightfall. The force numbered five infantry regiments, most of them hot-blooded Walloons – about 3,000 men with regimental guns and six field cannon. Reinach had left Halle at dawn and slogged the 30km down the narrow lanes as fast as his cumbrous artillery would allow, keen not to let Pappenheim down. At about 2.00pm the force encountered routers from Bönninghausen's cavalry regiment, who announced that their beloved Field Marshal was dead. Reinach refused to believe them and pushed on.

When Reinach's force finally reached the field, their hackles were up. Even though it was already dark, they marched straight for the Swedish positions. Seeing them advancing with intent to restart the battle, Holk rode up and shouted, 'Halt! Halt! What do you think you're doing?'

Wallenstein was convening a meeting of the senior surviving officers, and Holk urged Reinach and his colonels to attend. In the meantime Reinach sent Augustin von Fritsch, a junior officer of the colonel's company of his regiment, to inspect the guns of the main Imperial battery. Fritsch left a fascinating account of his little adventure, in which he was accompanied by a trusted corporal.

'We got up to the windmills creeping on all fours, and since all was very quiet we stood upright and looked over the whole field as far as we could see – which, however, because of the darkness of the night was not very far.' For a time Fritsch was in fear for his life, believing he could make out the glowing match-cords of Swedish muskets. 'I saw, however, that they were only candles which the soldiers were holding as they looted the battlefield or visited the dead. From there I went over to see our big cannon, but there was not a single soldier of ours or the enemy's at that place. I went back via the windmills to the General [Reinach] and told him everything – that Wallenstein's guns stood just behind the windmills, and if only we had the horses and harness to service them, we could easily tow them off.'

In the meantime Wallenstein's impromptu conference had reached a conclusion. The colonels of Reinach's infantry and Wallenstein's surviving colonels had voted unanimously to push in another attack. But Wallenstein vetoed them, and decided to abandon the field and retreat to Leipzig. It took all of Holk's tact to restrain their frustration. Moments later Fritsch arrived with information about the heavy guns. It made no difference: Wallenstein had made up his mind. Preparations were being made to leave the field silently without alerting the Swedes.

Why did Wallenstein decide to retreat? The Imperialists had not 'lost' the battle. Most of his troops, except the few cavalry regiments that had routed earlier in the day, were still on the field. The baggage wagons, though lacking drivers, were still half full of ammunition. Despite the death of Pappenheim, his fresh infantry were now on the field, commanded by Reinach and eager to fight, giving Wallenstein the means to continue the battle into a second day.

Officially it was the strategic situation that forced Wallenstein's hand. Holk later wrote that, 'The Duke [Wallenstein] … considered it better to march off … and combine with Gallas's corps before the Saxons could join with the Swedes.' Wallenstein, having seen the appalling casualties his men had suffered in the roll-call returns from his regiments, expressed concern that his troops were in a 'desperate state' and would not be able to face a second day of combat. It was another bitterly cold night, and he was also worried that many soldiers would sneak off to find shelter, and not be around to fight in the morning.

Having lost a large part of his force, relatives (his cousin Berthold, his brother-in-law, Count Harrach) and friends (including Pappenheim) Wallenstein was far from emotionally unaffected. A bruise on the thigh from a spent musket ball was a reminder of his own mortality. Wallenstein was as physically and mentally shattered as were his troops. The simple attraction of a warm bed in Leipzig should not be underestimated.

By calling a retreat Wallenstein was cutting his losses. Undoubtedly the biggest sacrifice was the artillery, for which he no longer had draught animals. The gamble of mounting his baggage boys and camp followers to plug the hole on his left wing at the start of the battle had backfired. Most of the army's baggage was also left behind, along with 20 wagon loads of unused ammunition.

The retreat began 'three hours into the night' or about 8.00pm. Wallenstein, Holk, the two young Medici dukes, together with Colloredo and Grana left the field between 9.00 and 10.00pm. Pappenheim's infantry covered the retreat, before following themselves. Hofkirchen's regiment was instructed to stay behind with the rearguard, but again disobeyed orders and joined the retreat. The field was left to the Croats and local farmers, who went about looting the dead. In revenge for Holk's marauding, the farmers killed any Imperial wounded and stragglers they found.

Wallenstein reached Leipzig soon after midnight along with about 80 horsemen. Holk and a number of other senior officers arrived soon after and found quarters. Later, in the dead of night, the bodies of the Prince-Abbot of Fulda and Pappenheim were carried into the Pleissenburg castle, where, to the disgust of the worthy Saxon burghers, Pappenheim's corpse was embalmed on the main dining table.

The loss of the artillery meant that Wallenstein no longer had a viable field army. With the campaigning season drawing in, it was, anyway, time to think about winter quarters. Wallenstein decided to abandon Leipzig on the 18th, and the same morning his troops began to march out of the city southwards towards Borna and Grimma, the priority being to join with Gallas, the ultimate destination being the safety of Bohemia – for Wallenstein, home.

A gallows to the rear of Wallenstein's army appears on several paintings and prints, but may have been borrowed in error from maps of Breitenfeld. A similar legend surrounds an explosion that is said to have destroyed part of the Imperial ammunition. In fact Wallenstein was never short of gunpowder, and large quantities were captured by the Swedes after he abandoned the field. Detail from Jacques Courtois' painting of the battle. (Pitti, Florence)

A curious victory – the Swedish army after dark

As night fell Bernhard's infantry held the windmill battery. Capturing it had been appallingly expensive, but the position was too exposed to risk holding overnight. Reluctantly, Bernhard ordered his soldiers to pull back, leaving behind the Imperial guns they had spent the greater part of the day fighting to take. Most of the Swedish wagons had fled back towards Naumburg in fear of the Croats, so few provisions were available that cold night, and the men remained hungry and thirsty. The regiments 'lodged in the formations that they had held during the day'. Another day of battle seemed inevitable, and it was important to be ready for action at first light.

An empty, inconsolable sadness at the loss of the King had descended upon the Swedish commanders, and it would appear that Bernhard and Knyphausen, far from celebrating victory, were making plans to retreat. With little ammunition in the few remaining wagons, the army probably did not have the means to fight a second day.

Fortunately, news came of Wallenstein's withdrawal after the capture of a straggler from Hofkirchen's (Sparr's) horse regiment. There would be no need to retreat after all. A message to Oberst Henderson countermanded an earlier order to destroy the Imperial cannon (probably of the ditch battery). It reached him after he had burnt only one or two of the gun carriages. (*The Swedish Intelligencer* 3, 151)

The Protestant soldiery awoke on Wednesday morning, 17 November, still in the battle formations of the previous day. A glance northwards showed that the Lützen plain was empty except for a few companies of Croats, scavenging among the debris of battle. The town of Lützen had been reduced to cinders, only the castle was still standing.

Öhm's cavalry regiment, which Knyphausen had kept in reserve all day, was sent to chase off the Croats and find the enemy. Swedish officers were soon up by the windmills examining the cannon of the main Imperial battery. Bernhard ordered each cavalry regiment to supply horses to move the pieces to the courtyard of Lützen castle and posted 200 musketeers to guard them. A single damaged 24-pdr remained on the field until a replacement carriage was found later in the day.

With the threat of action passed, the Swedish Army now seemed in danger of lapsing into chaos. With numerous officers wounded or dead, the ordinary soldiers (noted the King's secretary, Philipp Sattler) began 'stealing off in all directions, under the pretext of treating their wounded comrades'. The flight of the Swedish wagons meant that ammunition and provisions were short, so pursuit was out of the question. A brief staff conference concluded that the only sensible option was to retire to the camp at Naumburg: to put the army back in calmer order, to feed the troops and to allow a proper night's rest.

At about 10.00am the Protestant army formed up on the battlefield, and at 11.00am began its solemn march back to Weissenfels. Rumours of the King's fate were circulating, but most soldiers still did not know whether Gustav Adolf was wounded or dead. When the army had reached Weissenfels, Duke Bernhard assembled the officers and broke the news to them: the King had been killed.[14] Bernhard asked for support in continuing the campaign under his personal leadership; his officers gave it unequivocally.

After being removed from the battlefield late in the afternoon, and resting briefly in Meuchen church, the King's body had been secretly

THE IMPERIAL RETREAT

Wallenstein's decision to retire from the battlefield came as a surprise to many of his troops, who believed the battle had not gone too badly and would continue into a second day. The retreat towards Leipzig began three hours into the night (about 8.00pm) 'without either sound of Trumpet or Drumme' to alert the Swedes, and continued into the small hours. Morale was rock bottom, especially in Pappenheim's corps: 'We marched with our heads down like gypsies, some regiments with but 100 men by their colours …' Most regiments were quartered that night in the suburbs of Leipzig. (Graham Turner)

transported to Weissenfels where, in the Geleitshaus (traveller's house), it was embalmed by a local physician. Swedish officers were later admitted to pay their respects. When, after a few days rest and reorganisation, the Protestant army was again ready to march, the King's body in a funeral casket took its place in the march column, between the infantry and cavalry, still symbolically in command of the army.

WHO WON THE BATTLE?

As night fell neither side knew or really cared who had won the battle 'so tired were they of the game', as Holk admitted. The battle had been hard fought, but because of the mist and smoke and fall of darkness few soldiers had an overall picture of how the battle had progressed and who deserved the victor's laurels. The Imperialists had seen the destruction of the Yellow and Blue brigades and the flight of Bernhard's cavalry and believed, quite justly, that they had got the better of the close-in fighting. The Swedes for their part had enjoyed many local successes, had nearly broken both Imperial wings and had taken both Imperial batteries, and at the day's end were left in possession of the field.

Although in the longer term Lützen was acknowledged as a Swedish victory, many Imperialist officers continued for several weeks to claim that they had won the battle. Wallenstein had certainly not done as poorly as Protestant historians later made out. Indeed by conventional measures of victory, one could argue that Wallenstein won the tactical battle of Lützen.

Since battle casualties were rarely counted in this period, the most tangible signs of victory were the flags taken from the enemy, which gave a direct count of formations broken up. In these terms, the Imperialists came off rather well. On the day after the battle, Wallenstein wrote: 'I took from the enemy over 30 standards and colours, he got from me no more than five or six at the very most.' Wallenstein gave out cash rewards for 34 captured Swedish flags: Comargo's regiment was credited with ten infantry colours and Baden's two, Kehraus' got four, the three Breuner regiments got seven between them. Eight cavalry units got an infantry

ABOVE, LEFT **Bombardment of the Pleissenburg in Leipzig. Wallenstein left Leipzig on 18 November, after putting a 600-man garrison in the town's Pleissenburg castle. Its recapture was entrusted to the Saxon General-major Lorentz von Hofkirchen. Despite heavy shelling the fortress held out for three weeks. (Germanisches National Museum, Nuremberg)**

ABOVE, TOP **In places on the battlefield the corpses are said to have lain 'half a man high'. Three hundred bodies were found in and around the walled gardens near Lützen, the scene of some of the day's heaviest fighting. The fallen Protestant officers were buried with honours in Lützen churchyard, the ordinary soldiers were tossed unceremoniously into the ditches alongside the Leipzig road and covered with soil. Detail of a painting by Jan Martsen de Jonge dated 1634, showing Gustav Adolf in battle. (Stockholms Slott)**

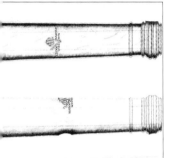

ABOVE **Among the captured Imperial guns were ten splendid demi-culverins (24-pdrs) embossed with the Imperial eagle and Emperor's name. Most of Sweden's artillery trophies were long ago sold off for scrap, but these drawings made in the Bohus fortress in 1691 by artillery captain Johan Kirsten, may show Lützen guns. The two 24-pdr barrels were cast in Vienna in 1628 and 1630. (Ritningssamling, Kungl. Armémuseum, Stockholm)**

colour and/or a cavalry cornet a piece. For some reason no payments were made for the 'remaining cornets (taken) by Piccolomini's, Bredau's and Trčka's (horse) regiments'. Diodati commented that many Swedish flags were left in the field because little more than bare staffs remained. By his estimate, the total of Swedish flags taken was 60.

For their part the Swedes took no more than a dozen flags, most of them from a single Imperial horse regiment, Hagen's. (Gustav Adolf's haul at Breitenfeld had been 19 cavalry standards and 80 infantry colours.) Holk admitted losing up to eight cavalry cornets, but insisted that 'not one infantry colour was lost'. According to one broadsheet Bernhard was later presented with 28 cornets and about 50 colours – 'but because of the doleful fate of the glorious king and leader, little attention was paid to such matters'. These flags were almost certainly taken in mopping-up operations and not at Lützen itself.

This disparity in the numbers of trophies can to some extent be explained by the different combat styles of the armies. The Swedes relied heavily on distance weapons – muskets and cannon-fire; the Imperialists won far more trophies by combining infantry and cuirassiers to demolish enemy formations in hand-to-hand combat.

SWEDISH INFANTRY CASUALTIES BY BRIGADE

Swedish Brigade	Original strength excluding officers (1)	Final strength excluding officers (2)	Listed as wounded, excluding officers (3)	Killed, wounded or unaccounted for
Swedish	1335	874	374	35%
Yellow	1017	324	273	68%
Blue	918	331	381	63%
Bernhard's	1560	958	223	39%
Wilhelm's	1440	1192	62	17%
Knyphausen's	978	769	96	21%
Thurn's	1260	1068	33	15%
Mitzlaff's	1500	930	254	38%
Henderson's (4)	978	600	230	39%
Totals	10,986	7,046	1,926	36%

(1) Source: Langman's list, 14 Nov. 1632 (see notes to Swedish orbat).

(2) Undated list of the regiments shortly after Lützen: GA verket, vol 32d, List 2.D.20, Krigsarkivet, Stockholm.

(3) *Arkiv till upplysning om svenska krigens ... historia*, III, No. 946 (Stockholm 1861). A further 400 wounded officers and soldiers were quartered in Weissenfels.

(4) Including Löwenstein's and Brandenstein's regiments which were deployed as commanded musketeers.

The Swedish estimates for their own casualties suggest about 1,500 dead and 3,000–3,500 wounded. The Swedish chancellery estimated 100 officers killed or seriously wounded. A detailed list of the infantry wounded was made after the battle: this accounted for 2,200 men and officers, and a further 400 were said to be lodged in Weissenfels. Unfortunately, no list of the cavalry casualties survives. The number of deserters is difficult to tally, but when Bernhard reassembled the army at Naumburg, it was found to number 12,000 – no less than 6,000 short of its pre-battle strength.

The Imperial losses are more difficult to gauge since they abandoned the field and therefore many of their wounded. Cynically Wallenstein left behind a further 1,160 wounded in Leipzig, most of them captured when the Saxons retook the town. Historians have always assumed that the Imperial casualties were heavier than those of the Swedes. But Swedish estimates were grossly exaggerated for propaganda purposes. The most

Der Schwede lebet noch.

'The Swede lives on,' a German print dated 1633. Gustav Adolf stands on three crowned mountains (the Swedish coat of arms), while a six-headed dragon (the Imperial cause), swims the chaotic seas of Germany. The combination of the Swedish arms (on the shield at left) and the Saxon arms (at right) announce the most important result of Lützen – that the Swedish–Saxon alliance remained intact.

reliable Imperial sources, Holk and Diodati, settle on a figure of just 3,000 Imperial dead and wounded. Even if this is too low, other estimates seem to confirm that Imperial casualties were significantly lower than those of the Swedes.

That the Swedes sustained higher casualties is only common sense. They had assaulted a partially entrenched position under heavy fire in the hope of dislodging Wallenstein before Pappenheim arrived. The Swedish infantry brigades were cut to ribbons during these repeated assaults. Knyphausen's secretary, Christoph Milde, believed 'it was the cannon in particular that caused the great damage to both sides'. Yet the Swedes did not have all their heavy cannon on the field until at least midday.

Wallenstein undoubtedly got the better of the fighting, but he blotted his copy book by abandoning the field, his artillery and ammunition, turning a tactical victory into a strategic defeat. The Protestants, aside from eliminating the troublesome Pappenheim, achieved their main goal of the campaign: Wallenstein had been forced out of Saxony and back to Bohemia; and most importantly, Johann Georg of Saxony was again back in the Swedish fold, at least for a time.

In the longer term though, Lützen was a Protestant disaster: Gustav Adolf's death deprived the Protestants of the moral high ground – the German crusade was over. Although cracks in Gustav Adolf's relationship with the German princes had appeared, he had been the only person able to unite the disparate factions and bring the war to a rapid conclusion. The death of the Lion of the North was equivalent to the loss of tens of thousands of soldiers.

It is possible, then, to argue that Lützen was simultaneously a tactical victory for Wallenstein and a strategic one for the Swedes. In a broader sense though, both sides lost the battle of Lützen.

Lessons learned

The battle had shown up a number of shortcomings in the Swedish military system. The Protestant cavalry had not performed well, as Colonel

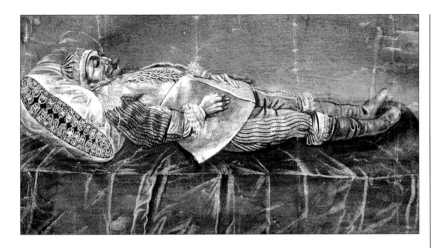

Fleetwood commented: 'Had not our foot stood like a wall, there had none of us come off alyve … our horse did but poorely.'

Count Nils Brahe's sibling, Per, complained that his brother's infantry brigades had taken heavy loss because 'our cavalry provided no support'. Fearing the Imperial cavalry, Gustav Adolf had denuded his centre of cavalry to strengthen his wings. Watts makes clear this error of deployment in his comment that the Swedish Brigade escaped lightly because it was closer to the cavalry of the right wing. The Swedish brigade formation was also partly to blame for the defeat. It was too complicated to use in attack, its inherent weaknesses laid bare in the chaos and smoke of Lützen. Small wonder then, that within two years of Gustav Adolf's death it vanished from the battlefields of Germany.

The battle also exposed weaknesses among the Imperial troops. Wallenstein noticed that the cavalry that had taken part in the *Fahnenflucht* had been inadequately armoured. In memos sent in January 1633 to Gallas, Holk and the Bavarian general Aldringen, Wallenstein proposed a remedy: 'In the battle of Lützen the difference between armoured and

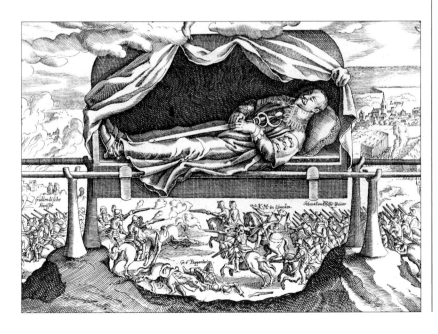

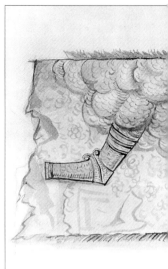

unarmoured cavalrymen came clearly to light; the former fought, the latter took flight. Therefore over the winter, all colonels should equip their cavalry with cuirasses.'

Furthermore Wallenstein proposed to stamp out the use of carbines by his German cavalry – the last vestige of the caracole: 'After shooting they turn their backs, which causes much harm.' He had also noted that his infantry officers had taken heavy casualties, which had a devastating effect on the morale of their troops. The remedy was to encourage them to wear adequate armour in battle. These instructions, Wallenstein added, were to be 'passed down to the regiments and carried out in reality'.[15]

Rewards and promotions

Wallenstein rewarded his men with customary liberality. As Holk, who was promoted to Feldmarschall, related in his account of the battle: 'The wounded received two months' pay, everyone else one month; officers got thank-letters and gold chains, others were advanced and a few ordinary troopers and musketeers were elevated to the nobility; gifts, depending on the status of the recipient, were 400, 600 and 1000 Gulden.'

Piccolomini, in particular, was showered with accolades. He later wrote (with characteristic immodesty), 'If two other regiments had done what I had, the enemy would have been completely ruined.' He was promoted to General-wachtmeister; his horse regiment (technically still a harquebusier unit) was officially upgraded to cuirassiers; and he was commissioned to raise a second cuirassier regiment and given a dragoon unit as well.

Knyphausen's cool nerves helped save the day for the Swedes. In a letter to the Swedish Senate the King's secretary Philipp Sattler noted that Knyphausen had 'done the most to sustain the wavering battleline'. His reward was the rank of Field Marshal (January 1633) and an independent command in Pappenheim's old haunt, the Lower Saxon region.

Bernhard was now de facto field commander of the Swedish Army. This became official when Duke Wilhelm of Weimar handed over his general-leutnant's baton to him soon after the battle. Later in 1633 Chancellor Oxenstierna gave him the duchy of Franconia, created out of the former catholic bishoprics of Bamberg and Würzburg.

ABOVE **The most important Swedish trophy from Lützen was the so-called Mainz Life-standard, taken from Hagen's regiment, which was regarded as a holy relic because of its links with Hagen's uncle, the former Archbishop-Elector of Mainz, Johann Schweikhard von Cronburg. It is of white damask silk and bears a distorted form of the archbishop's motto: SPES MEA CHRISTUS (Christ is my hope), above Christ crucified, flanked by Mary and St. John (the archbishop's first name). The reverse shows the arm of God emerging from a cloud. The finial is shaped as the six-spoked wheel of Mainz. (Swedish Trophy Collection, ST18:5)**

TOP, LEFT **Holk's prodigious exertions at Lützen greatly reduced the scale of the Imperial defeat. As a reward he was promoted to full Feldmarschall on 31 December 1632. Wallenstein was especially aggrieved when his energetic military technician was struck down during a plague epidemic at Troschenreut near Gera in Saxony on 8 September 1633. This contemporary broadsheet shows Holk 'giving up the ghost', while his infamously booty-laden soldiers look on. (Germanisches Nationalmuseum)**

ABOVE **Oberst Lothar von Bönninghausen was one of the key culprits of the Imperialist *Fahnenflucht*, but thanks to his connections (Holk in particular) was able to escape court-martial. However, his lack of valour soon became a popular joke. In this detail of a satirical broadsheet made after the Imperial defeat at Hessisch-Oldendorf in July 1633, he is shown departing the battlefield early 'to reserve quarters in Minden'.**

The question of what role the Swedes were to play in Germany was eventually decided in April 1633, when Oxenstierna was made Director-General of the Heilbronn League, a new organisation partly intended to replace the long-defunct Protestant Union. The Dukes of Brandenburg and Saxony declined to join.

EPILOGUE: THE *FAHNENFLUCHT* TRIALS

From 21 January to 11 February 1633 in Prague a gruesome epilogue to the Lützen battle took place, with the court-martial of the Imperial officers who had fled in the battle. Rumours circulated that the Saxon General-major Lorenz von Hofkirchen would attempt to rescue one of the accused, his brother Albrecht, oberstleutnant of Sparr's regiment, in an armed strike. No chances were taken: the town gates were shut and three infantry regiments were drafted in as guards.

Wallenstein pressed for the highest penalties, especially for Johann Nicholaus von Hagen, whose flight had taken place in full view of the generalissimo. A member of one of Germany's most respected families and a high-ranking knight of the Teutonic Order, his connections were insufficient to assuage Wallenstein's wrath. Hagen, Hofkirchen, ten other officers and five rankers were found guilty of cowardice. Only the oberstleutnant of Lohe's regiment was acquitted – the death of his colonel proof that the regiment had not retired without a fight.

The executions took place in the old town square of Prague. Parallels with the execution of the rebels of 1620 escaped few. One by one the sentenced men were led to the scaffold, forced to kneel and beheaded with a sword. Two men found guilty of looting their own baggage were sentenced to the less honourable death by hanging. Some of the condemned put on a brave face; others had drunk themselves into numbness; one fainted and was executed while unconscious. One artillery captain, openly defiant, refused attention from a priest (as a surprising number of them did), furious that his young son had been allowed to watch.

The reaction of the public was not one of bloodlust, but rather of horror at the human tragedy being played out before them. In the audience were many soldiers who had witnessed the violence at Lützen but could see no sense in this butchery. Most sympathy fell to Count Hillmair Staitz von Wobersnau, a handsome 19- or 20-year-old, 'of great worth and of the highest blood'. Originally timed to be executed fourth, he was kept back to the end in the hope that Wallenstein might listen to pleas for clemency. By the time he rose to the scaffold and stripped to the waist, the platform was slippery with blood. Piccolomini attempted to intercede with Wallenstein, his Italian temperament getting the better of him: 'Surely you can spare this one.' The audience echoed his call. Wobersnau faced his fate stoically, and addressed the public: 'I am not afraid to die, nor had I been so on the battlefield. I simply followed my colonel.' His voice was drowned by a drum roll, as the executioner's sword struck.

---

14 Richelieu's memoirs, p.262
15 *Documenta Bohemica Bellum Tricennale Illustrantia*, V, Prague 1977, Nos.321 and 324. The instruction about carbines implies that caracoling with pistols was no longer a problem. The non-German cavalry, i.e. the Croats, were exempt from this order.

THE BATTLEFIELD TODAY

A visit to the Lützen battlefield in former East Germany presents few of the problems that it did before 1989. Modern Lützen is an unassuming town of 3,000 inhabitants in the province of Sachsen-Anhalt, 20km south-west of Leipzig and 160km south-west of Berlin. With the rebuilding of the East German Autobahn network, road access is now straightforward and the battlefield is visible from the Berlin–Munich Autobahn (A9), which also crosses over the Rippach stream. Local buses run directly to the battlefield memorial from Leipzig and Weissenfels.

Although something of a 'Gustav Adolf' industry has developed in recent years, the key sites around Lützen can be seen in a day. The first port of call is the **Gustav-Adolf-Gedenkstätte (Memorial site)**, a 1km walk (or bus ride) north-east of the town along the Leipzig road, now aptly renamed Gustav-Adolf-Strasse. The site centres on the **Schwedenstein**, a stone said to mark the spot where Gustav Adolf was killed. Over the centuries the place has blossomed into a little piece of Sweden in Germany. Behind the Schwedenstein is the **Gustav Adolf Memorial Chapel** built in 1906, the destination of annual pilgrimages by members of the Swedish royal family (on 6 November), and worth a peek for the stained glass coats-of-arms of Swedish participants of the battle. A nearby 'Swedish house' promotes Scandinavian folklore and crafts. The 400th anniversary of Gustav Adolf's birth in 1994 saw the opening of a **Battlefield museum** at the memorial site. Sponsored by the Livrustkammaren in Stockholm, it houses pictures, maps and even a few battlefield artefacts.

The battlefield today, looking south-east from the old Leipzig road, with its single surviving drainage ditch in the foreground. This is the view that Imperial musketeers in the roadside ditches had of the advancing cavalry squadrons of the extreme right of the Swedish right wing. The complete lack of natural cover left the Swedes exposed to heavy casualties.

ABOVE **Lützen castle, to the south of the town centre, is the only building that was left standing in 1632. It houses the town museum, with a small section devoted to the battle, including a tin-figure diorama. Not to be missed is the 360° panorama from the castle tower.**

ABOVE, RIGHT **The Lützen-Leipzig road, which formed the spine of Wallenstein's position, was straightened in the 1790s, and further widened in the 1990s. The original road is now little more than a country lane, though it was once one of Germany's main highways. Note the drainage ditch on the road's south side. This, and a similar ditch on the north side (now filled), were dug out on the night of 15/16 November to make trenches for Wallenstein's men, the excavated soil forming a parapet.**

The battlefield has changed greatly over the past four centuries, and not for the better. The windmill hill, never a major geographic feature, was levelled long ago and the mills removed, and the whole western part of the battlefield is now covered by housing and supermarkets. The open fields over which the Swedish infantry centre advanced are completely obscured by a wood and nature park. In recent years, thanks to Swedish efforts and cash subsidies, the fields north of the Leipzig road have been protected from further development, so it is still possible to see the whole eastern part of the field, where Stålhandske's Finns advanced and Pappenheim was killed. About 1km further along the Leipzig road from the Schwedenstein is the **Flossgraben**, now little more than a stream that runs around the south and east of the battlefield. For those with more time and energy, a walk out south-east from the town, towards Meuchen, over the Mühlgraben and then north along the Flossgraben gives perhaps the best overview of the surviving parts of the battlefield.

Lützen town itself is disappointing, having been completely destroyed in the battle, except for the small castle. The **Castle Museum** is, however, well worth a visit. The town's oldest hotel, the *Roter Löwe* (Red Lion), renovated in 2000, has aspirations of becoming the main visitor centre and is reasonably priced. Bed-and-breakfast accommodation is also widely available.

The most interesting of several sites outside of Lützen is the **Geleitshaus Museum** in Weissenfels, where the King's body was embalmed after the battle. The room in which this operation was performed still has a fleck of the King's blood on the wall. Other nearby sites of Thirty Years War interest include Magdeburg, Dessau Bridge, Erfurt and, of course, Breitenfeld, just north of Leipzig. Napoleonic fans can also visit the 1813 Leipzig and Lützen battlefields. Colditz castle, of more recent fame, is also close by.

FURTHER READING

Most modern accounts of the battle derive from the Swedish General Staff's monumental 1939 study, *Sveriges Krig*. This has been partly superseded by more recent Swedish research, notably Cederström and Barkman.

German and Austrian accounts have often conflicted with the Swedish version of events, most noticeably Seidler, who in a series of articles claimed to have 'finally solved the Lützen problem'. His radically new (and somewhat haphazard) scheme of the battle, with Gustav Adolf dying near the windmills, aroused scathing criticism, but nevertheless influenced such reputable historians as Roberts, Mann and Barker. More recently Germanic historians have had a more critical approach: Holl and Stadler in particular have helped resolve the complex issue of the Imperial battle order.

Very few of the primary sources have been published in English, but Watts, Fleetwood and Poyntz all make an entertaining read.

Like Lützen, the Thirty Years War as a whole suffers from poor coverage in the English language. Wedgwood and Parker are the undisputed standard works. For military systems of the period Delbrück and Barker are rewarding, but require patient study.

Barker, Thomas M., *The Military Intellectual and Battle: Raimondo Montecuccoli and the Thirty Years War* (Albany, NY, 1975). A meticulous study of the influential general and his military manual 'On battle'. The account of Lützen is 'Seidler-ised'.

Barkman, Bertil Carlsson & Lundkvist, Sven, *Kungl. Svea Livgardes Historia*, Bd 3:1 (Stockholm 1963). A general history of the Swedish Lifeguard (former Yellow) Regiment, with a section on Lützen.

Cederström, Rudolf [ed.], *Gustav Adolf vid Lützen*, (Stockholm 1944). Lavish study of the Swedish King's death at Lützen, with the stress on surviving museum artefacts. The battle description is by Barkman.

Danielsson, Arne, 'Streiff, En häst till Hans Kungl. Majestäts behov', *Livrustkammaren* 12:7–8, p.215–17 (Stockholm 1971) About the King's horse, Streiff.

Delbrück, Hans, *The Dawn of Modern Warfare* (History of the Art of War, Vol. IV) (German edition Berlin 1920; American transl. by Walter J. Renfroe Jr., Bison Books, 1990). Outdated and cumbersome, but a gold mine of information on 17th-century warfare.

Fleetwood 'Letter from George Fleetwood to his father giving an account of the battle of Lutzen and the death of Gustavus Adolphus', *The Camden Miscellany*, Vol. I (London 1847) A garbled but honest eyewitness account by an English colonel in Swedish service.

Grimmelshausen, Johann Jacob, *Simplicissimus*. First published in 1669, several English translations available. The classic on soldier's life in the Thirty Years War.

Holl, Brigitte, 'Wallensteins angebliche Skizze für die Schlacht bei Lützen' in *Schriften des Heeresgeschichtlichen Museums in Wien Bd7: Der Dreissigjährige Krieg* (Wien 1976). Correctly identified the Weissenfels battle plan for the first time.

Mann, Golo, *Wallenstein his life narrated*, transl. Charles Kessler, (London: Deutsch, 1976). A tightly written classic, although as Mann freely admits, his account of Lützen is jumbled and incomplete.

Parker, Geoffrey (Editor), *The Thirty Years War*, 2nd edition, (London 1997). Concentrates on political and social aspects.

Poyntz, *The Relation of Sydnam Poyntz 1624-1636* (ed A.T.S. Goodrick) Camden 3rd series vol.14 (London 1908). Often unreliable account written down in 1636/37 by an English veteran of Wallenstein's army.

Preil, Arndt, *Österreichs Schlachtfelder Bd 1: Breitenfeld 1631, Lützen 1632, Breitenfeld 1642*, (Graz 1990). Useful modern photos of the battlefield, otherwise uninspiring.

Roberts, Michael, *Gustavus Adolphus, A History of Sweden*, 2 vols, (Edinburgh 1958). The most thorough English-language account of Gustav Adolf's career. The account of Lützen mostly follows Seidler.

Seidler, Josef, *Das Prager Blutgericht 1633* (Memmingen 1951); *Untersuchungen über Schlacht bei Lützen* (Memmingen 1954) and *Besteht noch ein Lützenproblem?* (Memmingen 1971) Seidler brought much new source material to light, but put far too much trust in second-hand accounts by 17th- and 18th-century historians.

Seitz, Heribert, 'Gustavus Adolphus's sword and the fatal shots', *Livrustkammaren* 16:1 (Stockholm 1982), p.22–31.

Stadler, Barbara, *Pappenheim und die Zeit des Dreissigjährigen Krieges* (Winterthur, Switzerland 1991). A solid, if somewhat lengthy, modern biography.

Sveriges Krig (by the Swedish General Staff) Vol. 6 Från Lech till Lützen, (Stockholm 1939). Colossal survey of the campaign and battle, not without errors.

Watts, William, *The Swedish Intelligencer*, Pt. 3, (London 1633). Compiled from eyewitnesses and European broadsheets, and though 'hypothetical' in parts, as Watts admits, it is the most detailed account of the campaign by a contemporary historian.

Wedgwood, C.V., *The Thirty Years War* (London 1938). Unravels the complex tapestry of events without sacrificing readability. Still in print.

INDEX

COMPANION SERIES FROM OSPREY

MEN-AT-ARMS

An unrivalled source of information on the organisation, uniforms and equipment of the world's fighting men, past and present. The series covers hundreds of subjects spanning 5,000 years of history. Each 48-page book includes concise texts packed with specific information, some 40 photos, maps and diagrams, and eight colour plates of uniformed figures.

ELITE

Detailed information on the uniforms and insignia of the world's most famous military forces. Each 64-page book contains some 50 photographs and diagrams, and 12 pages of full-colour artwork.

NEW VANGUARD

Comprehensive histories of the design, development and operational use of the world's armoured vehicles and artillery. Each 48-page book contains eight pages of full-colour artwork including a detailed cutaway.

WARRIOR

Definitive analysis of the armour, weapons, tactics and motivation of the fighting men of history. Each 64-page book contains cutaways and exploded artwork of the warrior's weapons and armour.

ORDER OF BATTLE

The most detailed information ever published on the units which fought history's great battles. Each 96-page book contains comprehensive organisation diagrams supported by ultra-detailed colour maps. Each title also includes a large fold-out base map.

AIRCRAFT OF THE ACES

Focuses exclusively on the elite pilots of major air campaigns, and includes unique interviews with surviving aces sourced specifically for each volume. Each 96-page volume contains up to 40 specially commissioned artworks, unit listings, new scale plans and the best archival photography available.

COMBAT AIRCRAFT

Technical information from the world's leading aviation writers on the aircraft types flown. Each 96-page volume contains up to 40 specially commissioned artworks, unit listings, new scale plans and the best archival photography available.